D0404496

strawberry & chocolate

strawberry & chocolate

SENEL PAZ

Introduction, translations & interview
by Peter Bush

BLOOMSBURY

First published in Great Britain 1995

Copyright © 1995 by Senel Paz and Peter Bush

The moral right of the author has been asserted

Bloomsbury Publishing Plc, 2 Soho Square, London W1V 6HB

10 9 8 7 6 5 4 3 2 1

ISBN 0 7475 23711

Typeset by Hewer Text Composition Services, Edinburgh
Printed in Great Britain by Cox & Wyman Limited, Reading

CONTENTS

'*Who the fuck's reading that pansy?*' –
Che Guevara on seeing a book by
Virgilio Piñera in the Cuban embassy
in Algiers, 1963, quoted in *Realms of
Strife*, Juan Goytisolo, 1990

'*I thought the fact that a peasant lad like
myself aspired to be an intellectual must
be the result of some subtle enemy
strategy.*' – Senel Paz, 1992

ACKNOWLEDGEMENTS

I was originally sent to the 1992 Havana Film Festival by Tariq Ali, the producer of *Rear Window*, a Channel Four series. I went with the idea of a documentary on Tomás Gutiérrez Alea and that quickly took shape after hearing Senel Paz and the director enthuse about their new project and encountering at first hand the interest generated in Havana by Senel's story. So my thanks to Tariq and to Alex Anderson with whom I collaborated in the making of that documentary. I would also like to thank colleagues at Middlesex University as well as Julia, Ruth and Tom who tolerated my various absences in Cuba. Amparo Lallana helped me transcribe the interview. María Diaz supplied the wonderful photographs of Havana and Senel Paz. I am grateful to Liz Calder for her eager support for Latin American literary causes.

Directed by Tomás Gutiérrez Alea – Juan Carlos Tabío
Screenplay Senel Paz
Director of Photography Mario García Joya
Edited by Miriam Talavera – Osvaldo Donatién
Music José María Vitier
Sound Germinal Hernández
Set Design Fernando O'Reylly
Costume Design Miriam Dueñas
Executive Producer Miguel Mendoza

CAST

Diego	Jorge Perugorría
David	Vladimir Cruz
Nancy	Mirta Ibarra
Miguel	Francisco Gatorno
Vivian	Marilyn Solaga

Produced by ICAIC(Cuba) – IMCINE and Tabasco Films (Mexico) and TeleMadrid & SGAE(Spain)

INTRODUCTION
By Peter Bush

Thirty years after the establishment of the UMAP (Military Units to Aid Production – a euphemism for military labour camps for homosexuals) and the turning into non-persons writers like Virgilio Piñera and Lezama Lima, the film *Strawberry and Chocolate* has become the most successful Cuban film ever in terms of audiences on the island. It has also won prizes abroad, a nomination for an Oscar for Best Foreign Film in 1995, been championed by Robert Redford and panned by leading gay critics. The latter claim the film patronises gays and is a propaganda coup for Fidel Castro's ailing regime because it gives an appearance of liberalisation from within. Why does a film about the relationship between a gay intellectual and young Communist militant, promoting the idea of tolerance, with lots of ironic, literary dialogue become a success with the mass of Cubans? Why is it slated rather than celebrated by queer theorists? This book makes available for the first time in English an interview with Senel Paz, his short story *The Wolf, the Woods and the New Man* and the original film screenplay of *Strawberry and Chocolate*. These are vital reading to understand his particular historical experience and the changes taking place in Cuban cultural life as the children of the Revolution explore the uncertainties of the present after enjoying the benefits of their revolutionary scholarships and healthcare.

Senel Paz has spoken of his project as a writer as an attempt to fill the imaginative void experienced by a generation which lived the days of the revolution as if they were attending 'a

weekend matinée performance'. That would also involve extending freedom of expression, for 'although total freedom of expression exists nowhere, one notices how capitalism cleverly creates the sensation that everything is possible, while we create the feeling that with socialism everything is impossible, except for those with official authorisation: you're never sure where you can go, where you can sit down, if you can move a chair, how many beers you can ask for, what issues you can tackle in your writing.' The freshness and irony of his work arise partly from his sensitivity to the sexual and political paradoxes, the intricate web of deception that distinctively mark out social relations, everyday communication, in Cuba. It is the freshness of perception of a rural outsider working the traditions of Havana.

The character David is central to his fiction for the page and the screen. He first appears in an early short story under a weeping willow waiting for the return of his long-lost father, an anxious vigil that leads only to disappointment as he doesn't merit a backward glance when father eventually turns up. He then goes to state boarding school in Havana and finds his heterosexual initiation haunted by the macho style favoured by his Communist Party mentors – *Don't Tell Her That You Love Her*. The pursuit of an authentic sexuality extends to other characters who move between films like *A Girl Friend for David* (1985, director Orlando Rojas) and *Delightful Deceits* (1991, Gerardo Chijona). The latter reaches its comic climax when the wife of a scriptwriter is overjoyed to confront her husband and mistress in a restaurant: her nightmare had been that he was having a homosexual affair with the film director he was wooing with a hopeful script. A quite different level of public impact and artistic endeavour then comes with *The Wolf, the Woods and the New Man* (1991) which develops into *Strawberry and Chocolate* (1993, T.G. Alea).

An early working title for the film was *Enemigo Rumor* (*Enemy Rumour*, the title of a book of poems by Lezama Lima) reminding us that in a country where the media are controlled by the state, rumours abound and can be lethal. In a country preserving the apparatus of a Communist Party, threatened by the US boycott and the demise of economic support from Eastern Europe and the USSR, whispered criticism may be deemed the weapon of counter-revolutionaries, real enemies of the state. Every street and block of flats has its Committee for the Defence of the Revolution spectating, recording; every hotel has its card-carrying manager and lift operator who may be policing the scene while organising the trade in sex for tourists. *Granma*, the official newspaper, assures Cubans life is hard, but keep sacrificing for a better tomorrow. The optimistic sloganising is muted but the tone is ever upbeat. Admission of past errors from the pinnacle of power is an occasional ritual. Critical artists like Senel Paz and Tomás Gutiérrez Alea nourish their work on such contradictions.

Here's a rumour about *Strawberry and Chocolate*: after the Central Committee private viewing of the film in the presence of Alfredo Guevara, director of the Cuban Film Institute, but not of Fidel Castro, the only comment came from an old militant on Diego sifting through his opera records and lamenting the predominance of Maria Remola in Cuba – 'We need other voices in the island'. The militant could see no need for other voices. A few days later, for a New Year present in the absence of a Cuban Christmas, Alfredo apparently received from Fidel a bottle of rum and a bag of black beans. He was subsequently invited to converse for hours with a Fidel who berated the mistaken repression of gays, called for mistakes to be rectified, but made no mention of a film on the theme currently showing to packed audiences from one end of the island to the other. Rumour thriving on lack of truth, the particular form taken within a society still controlled by a Party which closes ranks behind its Leader and defends with remnants of socialist rhetoric a Revolution hungry for dollars. My particular gossip-monger gave up believing in any rectification of mistakes thirty years ago.

The present short story and film are turning-points in Senel Paz's career. The story won him the Juan Rulfo Prize awarded in Paris by Radio France Internationale, the Mexican Cultural Centre and the Casa de América Latina. The screenplay won the prize at the 1992 Havana Film Festival sponsored by Madrid Television and selected by a committee chaired by Eduardo Galeano. This international recognition coincided with collaboration with the leading Cuban film director, Tomás Gutiérrez Alea. Senel's previous screenplays had been filmed by directors making their first films and his participation was minimal. Alea's style is collaborative. The pre-shoot period was marked by get-togethers at the Alea household with the leading actors, directors of photography and production, interested critics and intellectuals. During the shoot, days would begin in discussion with actors on the set; weekends would be set aside for longer stretches of creative dialogue. Dialogue was even more extensive because Alea had to undergo a serious operation for cancer in the early stages of production and Juan Carlos Tabío stepped in to co-produce, generously postponing the editing of his own film, *The Elephant and the Bicycle*.

Strawberry and Chocolate had immediate broad appeal in Cuba for the obvious reason that it addressed immediate realities frankly. The daily deceptions, frustrations and survival strategies are there in the ironic dialogue and contradictory relationships. Though set in 1979, every detail could belong to the present of the Special Period of severe austerity established to cope with the crisis provoked by loss of Soviet subsidies, on the eve of the mass exodus of raft people. The film is embedded in references silenced by the official media:

lack of food and basic commodities, pigs being carried up staircases, decaying buildings, the blackmarket, clandestine bars, empty shops. The landscape for human survival is recognisable to anyone who has slept a night in central Havana and listened to the cacophony of farmyard sounds not usually associated with urban life.

The central theme of tolerance built round the relationship between Diego and David is explored in the context of the issue of leaving or not leaving the island and the future of the Revolution. Diego is the defender of Cuban culture educating the young militant who has absorbed the line of the Revolution that has made a scholarship boy out of a peasant lad. He introduces David to the architecture of the city, the writers and musicians of the nation's past, the homosexual contribution to culture. David is won away from the dogmatic militancy of his student room-mate, Miguel, through a series of challenging conversations with Diego and a growing unease with the policing role being urged upon him by Miguel. However, Diego the sensitive defender of the national patrimony is driven out of the country by the state bureaucracy which cannot accept criticism. He is the victim of a tradition that sees homosexuality as betrayal – 'How can you trust anyone who is even unfaithful to his own sex?' asks Miguel. A true socialist is a Cuban nationalist and is heterosexual.

The film was released in an atmosphere of expectation, as Senel Paz describes in his interview. The short story on which it was based had been published in 1991. An immediate success in Havana, it was turned into at least four stage versions. By making Lezama Lima the central figure in Diego's panoply of Cuban homosexual heroes, Senel Paz links his fiction with the great Cuban writer who died in Havana in 1975 after being turned into a non-figure in public life. Lezama now enjoys a cult status in Havana with young writers alongside novelists who died in exile: Reinaldo Arenas, Virgilio Piñera, Severo Sarduy, and Guillermo Cabrera Infante who continues to live in London exile. Lezama edited one of the country's foremost literary reviews, *Orígenes*, and wrote a masterpiece of erotic baroque, *Paradiso*. The first edition was published in a short run in Havana in 1966 but was soon withdrawn from the bookshops because of its exuberant sexual imagery, and copies were famously distributed around the various cultural attachés abroad for disposal as diplomatic Christmas presents. The recovery of Lezama Lima climaxes in a banquet which Diego offers David based on a banquet from Lezama's novel. The quotations from the novel contrast with the politically correct subjects of David's writing – collective farming and struggling, striking proletarians – while the food consumed in the story and film contrasts with the meagre fare on offer to Cubans. It is a clandestine festivity costing a hundred dollars at a time when ordinary Cubans were forbidden to hold dollars and engineered by Nancy, who occupies a humble position in the neighbourhood surveillance network.

Expectation was heightened when it was known Tomás Gutiérrez Alea would direct. Alea is well-known for films which maintain a critical line although they are produced by the Cuban Film Institute that was established soon after the Revolution. Alea's films have suffered from being interpreted simply as being close to the Revolution: the director as critical apologist or fellow traveller. This is compounded by the difficulty of writing about Cuban culture which has been politicised in a particular way: emphasising either Alea's being 'within' the Revolution or his opportunism and cowardice. In fact, one could argue that Alea's films have become more and more critical and that all his films are being positively re-interpreted by young Cuban filmgoers and makers. *Strawberry and Chocolate* strikes a pessimistic parallel with Alea's most celebrated film, *Memories of Underdevelopment* (1968) because, unlike Diego, Sergio the petty-bourgeois intellectual anti-hero of the latter decides to stay in Cuba at the height of the 1962 missile crisis. It was made in 1968 when the government was pouring out massive propaganda to galvanise efforts to reach a harvest of 10 million tons of sugar – a target that was not met despite much individual sacrifice by thousands of Cubans. In that context the film came under fire from Party hardliners.

A later film (1971) – *A Cuban Struggle with the Demons* – is set in the seventeenth century. A priest in a coastal village is trying to defend his flock from foreign ideas brought in by pirates. He is opposed by liberal humanist and hedonist Juan Contreras, who insists on the right of people to enjoyment now rather than the eternal postponement of happiness. Alea often refers to this film as one of his favourites, partly because of sequences of poetic images, one of which has Juan Contreras descending into the mists of hell intercut with subliminal images of José Martí, Che Guevara and Fidel Castro in the Sierra Maestra to a sound track of *Vivas!* from the Plaza de la Revolución. After hearing a soothsayer's pessimistic prophecies, he leaves hell and rides back to the pueblo where the priest is haranguing his congregation. They should leave for the interior, build a new community and a new man – an obvious reference to the moral vision of Che Guevara. In other words, Alea has never been afraid to enter the most delicate areas of revolutionary truth in Cuba.

The interview, short story and original screenplay enable us to see how much of the film emerges from the personal experience and fictional worlds of Senel. However, particularly in the writing of the screenplay, he builds in references to Alea's *Memories*. The parallels between Diego and Sergio are plain enough despite the difference in artistic treatment and genre: the recent film is deliberately constructed as a popular film. There is for example the incident in *Memories* when Sergio is driving with his friend to the airport and says that 'These people like someone to think for them' just as they pass an enormous hoarding with an image of Fidel. The remark is echoed several times by Diego. Both films are about leaving or staying: Sergio stays, Diego leaves

In the movement from story to screenplay, there are several important changes. One is the location for Diego's Den. This was going to be in an old hotel served by a lift. The actual location is a building known as La Madriguera – The Rabbit Warren – in old Havana, a grand private house that became a boarding-house later transformed into popular housing by the revolution. What with the headless Delacroix-style female figure of Liberty on the main stairs, backed by a fading mural of revolutionary leader, Camilo Cienfuegos, beneath a gallery of Martyrs, the wrought-iron inner staircase, patio, fountain, and ubiquitous flaking plaster, the house is undoubtedly the perfect setting for Diego's melancholy tale of the twilight of a beautiful city and its revolution. Also, who can ever say what the film gained by being shot in this building in the presence of its inhabitants rather than in an empty hotel? They provided a warm, protective atmosphere for the development of the film's themes and a visual symbolism beyond the reach of any film studio as the realities of the physical and social edifice of La Madriguera entered and enhanced the fictions of the film. The production was literally born among lives which echoed its political and artistic nuances, its moments of material frustration.

Then, there are decisive changes in the relationships within the film. One of these concerns the character of Miguel – Bruno in the short story. Miguel's role in the film is cut back considerably, in what are the major changes to the original screenplay. The first long cuts are the scenes at the ballet where Miguel traps Germán, Diego's sculptor friend, in the lavatories and the main characters see a performance by Alicia Alonso, the doyenne of Cuban classical ballet. The second is in the scene where Miguel is being photographed by Diego. Both sequences underscore the repressed homosexuality of Miguel, the James Deanish Stalinist. One can only speculate on the reasons for these changes. Perhaps they are being reserved for the next novel? Perhaps they were thought to put too much emphasis on Miguel? That might overshadow the inner thoughts of the gentler David? Perhaps they would have over-politicised the narrative? Perhaps, as Senel suggests, they would have taken away from the central theme of the apprenticeship of the heterosexual in tolerance. Certainly, the setting in the Gran Teatro would have added visual variety. It is an important site for public gay activity in Havana and is an old, elegant theatre and the preserve of Alicia Alonso. But then it proved impossible to film there. The scenes were eventually filmed in the modern Karl Marx Theatre and finally not included. The other sequence would have heightened the repressed homo-erotic. So Miguel is partly lost while Nancy is retained.

Nancy, played by Mirta Ibarra, Alea's wife, establishes the predominance of heterosexuality in the triangle with David and Diego that is so disliked by gay critics. She is however central in establishing the popular melodramatic nature of the film. It is a role and a character already present in Senel's fictional world – Nancy appears even more hysterically in *Adorables mentiras*. She is then a character to help hook a mass audience into the serious subject. Her world of the blackmarket, prostitution, vigilance committee membership, *santería*–the Afro Cuban spirits and preacher she appeals to – are elements of local colour that go beyond the picturesque. They are familiar realities of everyday life suppressed from the official media, certainly in that particular combination.

Finally, to address critics of the film from outside Cuba.

The ingredients of this book show that the fiction and the film are genuine attempts to create works of art that are enjoyable and valuable as such but engage in critical political and social realities. If they do not match the call from queer theory or from political critiques made outside the island, one can only say that it is always easier to be correct from the outside, and that exiles do not have a monopoly of the truth, no more than do those who opt to stay inside. If an artist wishes to tackle the theme of tolerance for a mass audience, using a popularising art form, why not? When so much energy is devoted to the creation of theories of difference in matters ethnic, national, and sexual, why not accept there may be genuinely different possibilities of artistically exploring difference? Senel Paz's fiction and screenplays are helping extend the boundaries for critical discussion within Cuba.

SENEL PAZ
INTERVIEWED BY PETER BUSH
Havana, February 1995

PB: I was reading your story *The Weeping Willow*. There are cows and it's very rural. What's it all got to do with you?

SP: The cows are for real. I come from a family of agricultural workers, a very poor family which owned nothing and worked on the land and came originally from peasant stock. I spent my whole childhood in a mountainous region in the centre of the island. There aren't huge mountains in Cuba, but the Cambray range is the second highest. I lived in the foothills of the sierra; which was very beautiful, very unspoilt, very green with lots of animals. At the time, on my mother's side, the men worked on the tobacco plantations in the valleys. These plantations are also very beautiful, with rows of those huge-leaved plants. On my father's side, the men were basically cowhands, a bit like cowboys in Wild West films. I was brought up in these two worlds: both sides of the family worked on the land.

PB: When did you leave these valleys?

SP: We moved to a small village in 1958, just before the fighting in the war got very fierce. Partly because the war was being waged in the countryside and had reached the spot where we lived. But above all for economic reasons. We were living with my mother's family. My grandfather was the breadwinner. He was very ill and my mother became the head of the family. There's not much work for a woman on the land. We moved to a village where my mum began to work as a maid, a servant, until after a few years of the Revolution, she started to work making cigars. Tobacco has always been part of my life, though I've never smoked. And when we were in this village, the Revolution broke out and the village was liberated by Che Guevara's troops.

PB: What do you remember of the Revolution?

SP: Childhood memories . . . adults talking about the war, being frightened of soldiers and of Batista's police; it was a life of whispers, surrounded by danger, which we children thought very exciting, because you felt you were in a film, it was so tense. The attack on the village started early one morning, suddenly at three or four o'clock, the shooting went on for ages and was very loud. At dawn army planes flew over the village, but didn't in fact drop any bombs, although they did bomb other villages. It wasn't particularly difficult for the rebel army to take my village because government troops were concentrating on defending the city of Santa Clara, which was the provincial capital, and clearly our village was no important garrison. I remember everyone being very enthusiastic. It was like a fiesta, a carnival even before the war had finished. The Revolution was very important for my family, as I told you we were extremely poor and lived a hand-to-mouth existence. We hadn't started school. Illiteracy was the family tradition – perhaps an odd aunt or uncle could read and write with great difficulty.

PB: Were there books at home?

SP: No books at all. My four grandparents were illiterate, one grandmother could sign her name and count. My mum knew enough to write a letter, to read. And my prospects – and those of my sisters – were no different. The victory of the Revolution meant we were able to study, and I was in particular, because of the *machista* mentality of Cubans: my mother decided – my sisters being older than I am – that they should study a bit to secondary level, and then stop studying and work so I could keep on with my schooling. Obviously I think they made the right decision! And then I studied through the revolutionary government's system of scholarships until I graduated from university in 1973. I was the first person in my family to study at university and the first to bring books home. I made contact rather late in life with culture; the nearest I ever got was the radio, listening to novels on the radio, adventure stories . . . I saw my first film at the age of ten.

PB: Do you remember your first films?

SP: I can remember the first time I went into a cinema, I went with some friends, I was the youngest kid with some grown-ups and lanky adolescents. There was one cinema in the town. It had a very long auditorium with 700 or 800 seats, and high curtains as sidewalls and when we entered that darkness, my friends started tugging the curtains. I went underneath and felt the cinema was an infinite succession of rooms, one after another. And the film I saw, would you believe, was *The Werewolf* – that film where, when midnight strikes, the moon comes out and the man changes into a wolf; but even so the film didn't frighten me. I was dazzled by films. And almost immediately, my second or third films were *The Gold Rush* and *Modern Times*, which entranced me. Then I became a regular cinemagoer. Today it's difficult to credit, but my mother couldn't afford it. It cost twenty cents to sit in the stalls. There were three levels. Upstairs cost five and there were no seats, only long benches. My mother couldn't afford that. I remember she used to earn fifteen cents, and we paid eight on rent . . . My grandfather was seriously ill – he died two or three years later – and the whole family had to be fed. But at school they gave out free tickets for weekend showings to pupils who behaved well. I was wonderfully well-behaved! Every Saturday I went to the cinema, and sometimes in the evening . . . I had a friend who lived near our street and his parents had a bit more money and they gave him twenty cents to go to the cinema and instead of going in the stalls both of us would go upstairs. But my friend's taste in films was really bad. He liked blood and thunder films which I didn't really care for, but that's what he liked and he was paying. And we'd also have circuses, down-at-heel circuses, more like circuses for adults because there were lines that had a double meaning. I didn't have money to go to the circus either, and I didn't dare slip in for nothing like lots of people.

PB: What were these double meanings?

SP: Well, they were aimed at adults, dialogues with erotic references and jokes with swear words. It wasn't just a fairground type of circus but a bit like a review. I really was enchanted by the circus part. The one thing I wanted to do was join the circus. I was hypnotised by the circus and my first artistic ambition was born: I wanted to be a clown. Then there was a family in the neighbourhood which had a television, and some evenings they let some of us go and watch provided we behaved ourselves, and we used to sit in their living room, on the floor, and watch, among other things, a circus being shown on television. This is reflected in my first novel, *A King in his Garden*. I began to write scripts for a circus, a circus that was put on in the neighbourhood by five boys and two girls who lived nearby and we did every-thing, dance, acrobatics, everything possible, and the whole neighbourhood came to our circus routines. We sold bags of popcorn and it was a good laugh. We performed short comedy acts. I organised the whole script, I wrote comic interludes imitating what I heard or saw on the radio or television. Even lines with a double meaning . . . At about the same time I started to recite things in school assemblies, and to write short plays. Everything was going very well until some friends of my sister said one day that anyone who read poems in assembly or wrote plays was a *maricón* – a queer. I stopped doing those things.

PB: But then how did your writing develop?

SP: Although I wanted to write I didn't have any notion about literature or that you could become a writer, but I felt this great need to write. I always had good literature teachers, real lovers of literature, and they captivated me as well. Then at school, the schoolmistresses started to praise what I wrote and say that one day I would become a writer, that I wrote well . . .

At secondary school there was a literature teacher who, unlike the others I'd had, acted very coldly towards me. She was the daughter of the last mayor there'd been in the town; and I was from a poor background and my sisters were student leaders. So she looked at me from rather a political perspective. I thought she didn't like me and I struggled to write ever more beautiful essays, wanting her to take some notice of me. Because I really liked her: that infatuation a boy can feel for his schoolteacher. She had a really beautiful way of reading when she read a story, she'd finish it off; she was incredibly attractive and I wanted to win her over, I wanted her to take notice of me.

She taught me for a semester and the following semester went off to teach another class. And now I was taught by her sister who on the contrary did pay me some attention. And I kept writing essays and stories, tried to make them really good, hoping that she would talk to her sister at home and say, 'Didn't you notice how well this lad writes? He writes really well'. Then, years later, I found out that Arelis, as the teacher was called, always liked me. It was just an impression I'd formed. I wanted her to be too nice to me.

I began to read and began to write novels. I began to write before I ever got into reading and started to read through the school library. And so . . . I completed my secondary education, and came to study in Havana, with a scholarship, at what was then the only National School, where they gathered together the people with the best marks from all over the island. It was above all a school for studying science, but they chose their pupils on the basis of marks. I was very studious and disciplined and was consequently selected as I had some of the best marks in the whole province.

I was again lucky and had teachers who took my literary vocation very seriously, and began to guide me towards certain books, and I developed a more systematic approach towards literature. It also made me understand I had no talents in the field of science. I found it quite difficult to continue in this school with its emphasis on mathematics, physics, chemistry when I wanted to spend all my time reading literature.

It was then I began to discover films, theatres and get involved in the cultural life of the city. It was in this period at the school that *Memories of Underdevelopment* was being filmed and at the time, in about 1966, there were lots of children of agricultural workers, of people who had never studied and were studying for the first time. Many more from villages and the countryside than from cities. But there was the odd boy from the city, and I befriended the son of the great Cuban actress, Raquel Revuelta. He was in my class, and in the film, *Memories of Underdevelopment*, there is a moment in the adolescence of the main character when he goes to a brothel for the first time, and has an amorous relationship with a prostitute, and this boy looked a bit like the main actor and he got the part. You only really saw him from behind. It's more what he was looking at than what he does, and it was all down to having the right physique. And of course he exaggerated everything he did in the film, and we got to the scene in the brothel and none of us recognised him.

But the film was really interesting. I thought it sounded strange, that the title was a real disaster. But I waited for the first night with lots of enthusiasm and went to see it with high hopes, particularly to see my friend act. However, I really liked the film, it shook me. I'm not sure to what extent I understood it at the time. I liked it, and never imagined that I would eventually work with the same director. But I was never attracted to the cinema as a film maker but rather by the way films told stories . . .

By this time I had written three or four novels and had begun to win student competitions and my friends started to look upon me as a writer and I began to read them my stories.

PB: What has happened to these stories?

SP: I've got them hidden away somewhere. There's the odd paragraph that's still worth reading

PB: What were these stories about?

SP: They were very influenced by what I was seeing at the cinema and what I was reading. Lots of social comment, lots of social criticism. Some were very imaginative, almost fairy stories, and others were rather abstract. I don't know what happens elsewhere but in Cuba most writers go through a Kafka phase. When you discover Kafka, you start writing about that strange world. There were lots of films about non-communication – Bergman, Antonioni – that had little in common with our reality but they had their influence; I also wrote about non-communication, about other people being the problem.

PB: Apart from your studies, what was the move from the country to the city like for you and the others? Life became very different?

SP: Well, I missed the countryside and my family. I passed through the natural adolescent process of separating out from the family and taking my own decisions, and feeling fine. But in my case they were all women and my grandmother . . . We were always a very close-knit family, where we all loved each other, but we made the move from countryside to small town; first of all, my grandmother had never been to a small town; even today my grandmother has never been to Santa Clara, she's never travelled more than fifty kilometres; she's never been to Havana. She was a woman who had always lived in the countryside, and was worried about my mother leaving; mum had to go, she felt very protective towards us, and the idea of going away to school . . . We lived on a small piece of land. They'd barely let me go out of the door into the street; they didn't let me go out. I had to live in my imagination. I entertained myself. We lived in a kind of stable.

In Cuba, but particularly in the small towns, people mix a lot; I mean, you visit, you eat in other people's houses. There were only five boys and we got on very well. I never thought of myself as the leader, but to an extent we all lived in my fantasy; how should I put it . . ., my ideas, my creation, but directed by others, and we did things like making a rocket to go to the . . . fantasies all boys get into, right? But those circus acts . . . today when our neighbours reminisce about what we used to do, they say everybody enjoyed themselves. Because we were always inventing things, nothing dangerous, but imaginative entertainment that held the neighbours' attention; everything was invented in those backyards, where we had plenty of scope for action. The houses were in a very poor area, but there

11

was lots of space and trees, and we were in the middle of the countryside. And I hadn't abandoned the other part of my life; my family on my father's side still lived deep in the country, and I spent long periods in the countryside, where it was completely open; and rural Cuba isn't dangerous, no wild animals or poisonous snakes . . . My paternal grandmother had lots of sons, only sons, and she influenced my freedom differently. When I moved to the city, I came together with lots of other youngsters from the countryside; the majority were overwhelmed by the city and that didn't happen to me. I was totally tied to the land and rather than feeling upset at being away from the country, I began to feel very proud, and as it was a long way away, I started to be more understanding and loving towards it and feel constantly nostalgic. I wasn't very keen on city people, they seemed dangerous, always trying to deceive you, you couldn't trust them; peasants perhaps have more conservative values. I certainly didn't hanker after a life in the bars and clubs of Havana. What really attracted me was the cultural life, reading, books, theatre. The first time I went to the theatre, it was really extraordinary. And I went to the cinema and enjoyed the variety of films. But for the most part I wasn't overwhelmed by the city, or any building, but the technology, because for me everything was technology. I stayed in two schools, the one I told you about, that was semi-boarding, you could only get out at the weekends, and then I lived in houses which had belonged to the bourgeoisie that departed for the United States; in those big beautiful villas where we lived and which we destroyed because we didn't appreciate what was there. Until I came to Havana, I'd never experienced the pleasure of water on tap, or flush toilets. Flush toilets were what computers are now. They seemed really strange, and often I wasn't sure how to use them. And taking a shower seemed one of humanity's great inventions – and still does so today, whenever I have a cold or hot shower! That was city life for me.

When I went to university I had never used a telephone. I'd been studying in Havana for four years but all my friends were basically like me – from the countryside. Rather than making city friends, I made friends with people from outside. So I never needed to telephone anybody until I got to university. I remember how other students wanted to go to hotels, but I never felt that way, although I did go from time to time. And it always felt like this. When I went to the most sophisticated places in Havana, which was a city beginning to go down hill, I thought that automatic things wouldn't work for me, that doors wouldn't open – and it sometimes happened! One of the things we used to do at that time was to go to the Habana Libre and they'd let us go in the lift, up and down the lift, like it was an amusement park, and then you could boast you'd looked down on Havana . . . I'd go and visit my family a lot, whenever I had a two or three-day break. Until I got to university.

PB: How old were you then?

PS: Nineteen.

PB: How old were you when you came to Havana?

SP: I was fifteen. When I entered university, I'd never used the telephone, never worn a suit, never put a watch on, everything happened to me for the first time. Twenty was an age for first-timing. Also I thought the university was a mysterious place . . . When I came to Havana for the first time, it made more impact on me, seemed bigger, with more buildings than New York, where I went last year – that seemed small compared to my first impressions of Havana. I was dazzled for awhile and then got used to it. And yet I knew where to go in Havana to find birds. I really missed the contact with nature in the city.

PB: How did going to university affect you as a writer?

SP: I got a place to study journalism and not literature. I went through an experience similar to that of David in *Strawberry and Chocolate*. I wasn't aware of any vocation to be a writer. As a student I went to cultural events. My involvement in student organisations was always in literary and artistic areas. But when I went to university I thought, 'I've been able to study thanks to the government, to the Revolution, society has given me an opportunity'. Writing seemed a very selfish luxury, something very bourgeois; I was into something I felt was of no use to anybody. I was dogmatic and I felt this aversion, but it in no way turned me off literature. I also had a very ingenuous idea about writing; for me writing was all about making up stories. Today I've gone back to thinking that's true.

But during the Sixties, I lived the whole theory about the writer's commitment, and the duty of the intellectual. All those things were in the air and I felt drawn to what was called a Latin American vocation; particularly after the Congress on Education and Culture, that very militant policy, that put social duty, support for the Revolution first. I was never very keen on all that but it influenced me. And then what I was writing seemed quite weak. I never saw literature as a way to make money and get rich, or to become famous, although one might dream about such things; but it seemed a very individual, very selfish pleasure, just for myself, very egotistical. I thought I should be ashamed of myself. I had guilt feelings and thought, 'Well, if God has given me talents, why didn't he equip me to be a vet, to prospect for oil in Cuba, to make a useful contribution to society'. I really prevaricated about concentrating on being a writer.

Through gossip I picked up anti-intellectual prejudices. I thought intellectuals were self-centred, politically problematic, practically traitors; they left the country, didn't participate in socially constructive activities, didn't enthusiastically support the Revolution. They just put difficulties in its way: this was the idea floating around. They seemed dangerous, the kind of people I should have nothing to do with, because I was sure I wanted to put my country first, that I loved the Revolution. That was more important than they were; the feeling everything that happened in society was more important than a handful of individuals. I really believed all that, but I never stopped writing and reading. Then the Congress on Education and Culture came along, and started what we call here the Five Grey Years, and in fact I didn't like their policies or way of behaving, although I wasn't sure I understood or could defend literature, I felt that wasn't the way to go about things . . .

PB: What exactly was that policy like?

SP: It was a very extreme policy, an attempt to establish socialist realism in every branch of culture, I mean literature as an extension of politics, almost a pedagogical tool, and setting a norm about how one must write, about how things should be in order to have a predetermined function in society and siphon off things like feeling for language, complicated, doubting characters, who weren't always positive, themes that weren't social, that weren't historical; and I reacted to this situation by being inhibited. I simply stopped writing, though I still wanted to be a writer.

PB: Where did you go from there?

SP: In 1970 I met a writer, the first I had ever encountered in person. He was Eduardo Heras León, and he taught me at university, in the School of Journalism. In 1971 he had problems because of a book he had published, as did lots of writers whose works I was reading. They were punished and their books were banned. The same thing happened to writers from abroad, and I have to say I agreed with that to a point; I thought the arguments behind this policy seemed logical. We should defend our country, not let Europeans tell us what to do; all that nationalism seemed fine; but then I read the books, and couldn't find any of the terrible things being talked about. I didn't see the attacks were merited. As I didn't know any writers, I thought it was the writers who must be the problem, that they were CIA agents, they were two-timing, dishonest, but I didn't know a single writer. What's more they were religious; they were a bit like Diego. I began to run scared, and feel I wasn't on the right track. This wasn't what I should be doing, and, as I said, I didn't know any writers. But then I met Eduardo, and that was a friend-ship which brought lots of problems. It was a friendship that affected me and all his students. At that time I wasn't really active in the Communist Youth, but they expelled me. Eduardo's book was officially censured, and there was no way I could agree with that censorship. I knew him and couldn't believe he was the perverse character they were describing. I couldn't believe he was full of neo-ideas and cultural colonialism. I couldn't accept I was stuffed with foreign ideas, or that this man who was my teacher was – for I knew what he thought – that he was a man who . . . I thought they'd got it all wrong, but the people saying those things were politicians, revolutionaries. They were Party leaders, members, the youth, the government . . . people with a lot of authority in my eyes, I thought they must have made a mistake. I had two options . . . There was a lot of confusion and I thought there was something wrong with me; but I couldn't understand why they thought they must be right.

I finished my degree, graduated, and was expelled from the political organisation. I received some academic sanctions, but I finished and graduated, and by way of punishing me – I came out with one of the best degrees of my year – they sent me to work on a newspaper in the province of Camagüey. For some reason it was the place they sent anyone they felt they had to punish.

But as you can imagine, I'm from the provinces and it was no punishment. I wasn't particularly upset at being moved away from Havana. I went off very happily to work on a provincial newspaper. And I hadn't stopped writing during this period, I'd finished a book before I reached my twentieth birthday. Exactly a quarter of an hour before I made it to twenty! On August 29 I finished checking the book. It's a book bits of which are in *El niño aquel* and in my novel. And I did one of the daring things you do at that age – I sent the book off to the Casa de las Américas competition. They chose a story to put in an anthology and told me I was going to be published in their anthology. I went to the Casa de las Américas and withdrew my story: I didn't want to be linked to that world of writers and intellectuals. Then I was worried about the story and started to feel unsure about it. Writing for me was like taking the top of my pen off and water would gush out, a torrent of words, characters and situations, and I let it all come out, not worrying about structure or style, it was intuitive. Then I suddenly realised writing was more than the act of writing, that it was what interested me and something I had an awareness about. When I saw those pages of text, I felt respectful, and a sense of modesty, and I knew that I had to decide; on the one hand, I didn't want to,

I was a bit frightened about being a writer and accepting that, if I was a writer and published things, I would have to stand by them.

I had published a story in a university magazine, and people passed my stories around in the university, and I had this reputation as a writer, that I had promise, and even some writers read my stories. At the time I was really timid, not like I am now! I'd always lived in the countryside, and I'd only lived with women; my grandmother had this idea that women should walk on one side and men on the other. So my sisters walked together and I just walked with the animals. And then I had my own difficulties, not in relating socially with people, because I always got on well with people and always felt I was liked, but in getting involved in conversations. I always felt rather inhibited when it came to conversation.

I decided not to publish and to give up all this literature business and went back to Camagüey. I became an enthusiastic journalist but soon realised I wasn't really suited to journalism. I like journalism, the world of social communication, from a critical, theoretical point of view, and publishing magazines. But journalism, and particularly writing as a reporter went against my personality. I was never much interested in politics as such, or in politicians. I wasn't really interested in what this guy was doing, or thinking or what he thought yesterday or today, and how it all fitted together. As for being bold, a singer would turn up and you had to be the first to get there and interview him – that went completely against the grain. I always worked conscientiously. I struggled against my personality and struggled to get into places they were trying to keep you out of but even so . . .

I got on all right as a journalist because what I lacked as a reporter I made up for in my writing! I wrote and invented. So I decided I wanted to leave. I met a few writers who passed through the province, just a bit, never becoming real friends. I had to interview them and other leading lights in cultural life. Once, for example, I interviewed the musician Leo Brower, and he was a good contact. In Camagüey there's a ballet company, and I went to the ballet. It was a city with a level of cultural life and soon I made friends who wrote. This was towards the end of the Seventies when I decided to give up being a journalist and to become a writer. I had written thousands and thousands and thousands of pages. I went into one of those crises you get when you write and don't have any real contact with other writers, when you're isolated. I read everything I'd written and decided it was all terrible, hopeless and that I had to start from scratch. I almost binned the lot but saved some seventy pages which went into *El niño aquel*, and that's when I decided to return to Havana. That was very difficult. It took me a long time to find work, a place to live, in 1979.

I went in for the David competition run by the Writers' Union for unpublished writers, and the same year I managed the move to Havana. I arrived on 4 June and the prizes were announced on 16 June and I won the short story prize and the book was published straightaway and was well received by critics, writers and the general public. I began to meet writers and to feel as if I suffered with them, and the problems that weren't mine I began to feel as my own. I sensed that some people liked me and some didn't, but that now I was a member of the group. And so it went on till I published the novel in 1983. I decided to make a break. I think I'd had a very amateurish attitude to literature till then, I hadn't taken the profession of writing all that seriously. Now I had published two books relatively successfully. They'd been published, gone on the circuit, aroused interest abroad, the odd one was even published abroad; I thought I should take literature more seriously. I didn't react by writing and publishing more: on the contrary, it was a break point. I started to study literature more responsibly, in particular Cuban literature, where I had major gaps.

PB: Can we now talk a bit about how Cubans reacted to the film, *Strawberry and Chocolate*? Can you tell us something about expectations before the film was shown?

SP: I think there were more expectations of this film in Cuba than there had ever been of any previous Cuban film. My story was written in 1990, came out at the beginning of 1991, and was very popular. It's a story practically everyone has read. Young people and old and not just intellectuals. Lots of people have said to me, 'I don't usually read, it's the only thing I've read in the last five or ten years.' Lots of ordinary Cubans have discussed the story with me. I can say it's been very popular. Apart from the story, there is the issue raised and the writing, the issue and the creative act in both the story and the film go way beyond the established dogmas about what you can and cannot write inside Cuba. If you like, the story was the first step, but a short story can never have the immediate social impact of a film.

There were also several stage versions, four to be exact, and they had been very successful, and consequently people knew the characters and had opinions about how Diego should be played because at one point there were three stage versions being performed in Havana at the same time. All three were sold out and you'd hear people commenting, 'I prefer this David and that Diego'. It was just like the ballet. People went to see the different interpretations because everybody knew what the story was all about. Then when the news went round that it was going to be turned into a film, everybody was very enthusiastic, particularly about Titón (T.G. Alea) being the director: 'it couldn't be in better hands', they said.

I was very pleased that Titón expressed an interest in making this film because I felt he not only had great artistic talent, a sense of humour and the maturity to carry the project through, I also knew that he was a director with great abilities as a story-teller. There are many directors who are good filmically but can't narrate for the cinema. In Titón's filmography, narrative is very important, he can construct film narratives. So there were high hopes. Scripts sold for huge sums of money, and then people started to talk about actors, who was going to be Diego, because nobody ever imagined who might take that role. Everyone thought it would be someone older: between 30 and 35.

PB: How were the actors chosen?

SP: Jorge Perrugorría isn't a very well-known actor and he's much younger than he appears in the film. Titón had lots of sessions looking for the actor he had in his mind but this actor never showed up. Then it was decided to see whether Jorge could play the role of David and he came the same day as Vladimir: they were rivals for the part. He was a revelation to Titón who immediately thought, experienced director that he is, that he could have a go as the other character and he auditioned him. Jorge had been working over the last two years with a theatre director, Carlos Diaz, who really knows how to develop actors and Jorge had changed spectacularly. I'd seen him in various plays and had never taken any notice of him. In fact, I'd got this prejudice about him, that he was just a pretty face and I didn't rate him, I'd never been struck by him as an actor.

When Titón put him and another actor on his final short-list and invited me to the auditions to express my opinion and have my say in the final decision, I was quite convinced I would support the other actor, that I would try to make sure

21

it wasn't Jorge, because he didn't match my ideal. And when I saw them in the audition, I ended up supporting Jorge. I could see his potential, I felt he could take the character on . . . When the news got out, everyone was stunned, it was a real surprise. I think nobody but Titón could have chosen Jorge because they would have thought he wasn't capable of playing that role . . . People told me that, lots of people had preconceptions about the film and what Diego should be like. Because they were really familiar with Diego. That's what Jorge says in the documentary about the making of *Strawberry and Chocolate*. They think Diego is so and so, someone I know, other people think I'm him . . . There are at least 500 candidates for the part of Diego, not counting those who claim that they were Diego.

There was another comment which I found very amusing. Jorge is very good-looking and a girl friend of mine said, 'So they've chosen Perrugorría? Well, if David doesn't fall in love with him, he must be as hard as nails.' That's already a line on the story. People can't forgive David for being so sensitive and not falling for him. And others said, 'If he's going to play the homosexual, I'm turning homosexual.'

As I said, there was a blackmarket sale of the script. People really wanted to know what it was going to be like. I had made two films previously which hadn't really been shown much but there was interest in what my script was like. They said the first two scripts were made into films by directors directing their first films. Titón and Senel are a good combination. There was enormous expectation and the Cuban Film Institute was sensible enough to make sure there were no leaks, nobody connected with the film was allowed to see it. I saw it the day it was premiered. It was like a big sporting or political event. It was first performed in the Karl Marx Theatre that seats 5,000 and there were two performances. It opened the Havana Film Festival and there were lots of Cubans as well as

22

foreigners in the audience. I can't describe the atmosphere when the film finished: the applause, ovations, tears, joy, people leaping around . . . The fact is the film put the seal on so many things, on a tradition or way of doing things in Cuba. This had also happened with the story and that's why I think the story has been so important, not just because of the story it tells but because the short story and the film are clearly works of art which have been freely created and made on the island. We showed ourselves that it's possible to be much freer than we'd thought; that there were spaces we could occupy which we hadn't occupied. Lots of things had changed in our favour and we hadn't taken them into account.

So, that day, apart from raising lots of issues, the film made lots of people shed tears, as they saw justice being done, and, equally, the film won for intellectuals, writers, people in general, an authority, a space and an important voice. We'd all been speculating about whether . . ., there was always the risk with the film, and the short story, that it wouldn't be possible; it wouldn't be published; if it was, it would be a run of only 200 copies, the script would never be passed, the film wouldn't be shown, etc, we always worked in this negative atmosphere, and I think the film survived the tightrope. It never had any problems.

At the Film Festival, the film won the Jury Prize, the Audience Prize, and the Prize given by the Catholic Church. The film was born with every prize possible and a tremendous reception in the cinema. Even then people thought, 'OK, this is the Festival, but they won't let it be shown outside the Festival'. But it was shown in ordinary cinemas, everybody felt they had to see it and I think everyone did! For a long time it was the main topic of conversation: often lots of pompous things were said. But for writers it was as if you'd had stones in your shoes and had been able to get rid of them. Everyone felt a huge weight had been taken off their backs, because of what the film was about and because the film had been made in Cuba and because if we could make one, we could go on making lots more without being afraid, worried, without all that insecurity. I feel that people are very grateful that the film exists. As I said, people knew the story, they knew what it was about and that Titón was a great director and the very least they expected was that he would turn in a decent film.

REBECA CHAVES (Senel's partner): I've not spoken about this before. But I have this view of the film. I think that making the film was relatively trouble-free but there was often a lot of tension on the set; I think that Titón was always tempted and when Juan Carlos Tabío joined as co-director . . . the film was tempting for lots of people, lots of film directors, including myself. There were lots of directors who regretted they hadn't made the film. Once Titón was chosen for the key role, I think he was often tempted to push the film in particular political ways, and the film would have suffered. I think, in that sense, Senel acted as a kind of brake. I mean, it's not the same when one reads the text, we each interpret it through our own inner world, see it through our own eyes, as when one puts a frame on a particular image, and that image then determines, makes it concrete, gives it ONE meaning. But in literature that . . . I think that Titón was very tempted, and when Juan Carlos joined the filming, there were some very interesting discussions. Juan Carlos suddenly developed the theory that the person on Diego's altar, the central figure on the altar, should have been Fernando Ortiz – the great anthropologist and historian of Afro-Cuban traditions – and not Lezama Lima – the gay, Roman Catholic novelist, creator of the erotic masterpiece of baroque prose, *Paradiso*. For Juan Carlos that represented a whole line of thought, and Fernando Ortiz offered a range of cultural and narrative possibilities. And Juan Carlos wanted the relation between David and Diego to be much more ambiguous. I think he always found it very hard to understand that the film was – and I think the phrase captures the essence of the film – a film for heterosexuals. In other words, it makes no sense for Diego to convert David. It's not *The Kiss of the Spider Woman*. So there was always this temptation, and that temptation created . . . well, you were there at times when . . . Senel spent a long time reading that scene, but I would say . . .

SP: I had to defend my position in writing, that there should be photos of Lezama, partly because it was a time when I thought it would be persuasive to write things down and not talk them through, I wrote down a whole theoretical position . . . Both Titón and Juan Carlos are people who listen carefully to what their collaborators think. I was very much opposed to the change, to the changes that were introduced into the scene where Diego tells David he's leaving; and I think that the whole argument helped to confirm Titón of the rightness of his decision. I feel that I didn't waste the time I put into the discussions. He didn't go for my option but he became more convinced of his own position, after he'd analysed my arguments . . .

RC: I think that Senel was always, always, always . . . and this is something people don't . . . don't talk about, the context of the circumstances in which the film was made. What I mean is that the film was made in a race against time. It was a race against time, and it was surprising that Titón, as a cinema person, should put to one side the cinematic possibilities and make the film in a really literary framework. That surprised me from the onset. And then, when we were in the editing room, he was so tense in the editing . . . It became a struggle

25

against time, and I think it lacks . . . and I say this quite respectfully, I think that lots of people won't speak to you straight because people put the films you've made in the ranking you've given them, but I think films have to have the timetable they need, because one cannot write a film to be 90 minutes long, because if it's 92 minutes, so what, if it has to be 92 minutes? But I told him, I spoke to Senel about what Titón had done . . . I think that in this sense, it lacked a certain emphasis; if he had made the film in different circumstances, I think the editing would have been quite different; for example, the whole business about Havana didn't really gell; at the beginning of the film, it was all rushed; there's this hurried note throughout the film . . .

I think that Titón had his finger on the pulse of the reality we wanted to engage with. Then when you say to the cameraman – it's a translator's reality too – I remember an image that you've forgotten, that everybody's forgotten, that was of a bus which was really full, over full, and the bus left a stop and drove past a hoarding that said 'Everything we are, we owe to you'.

SP: It was a bus, and as it drove by, the slogan was in the background.

RC: That's a very strong image . . . it was a very harsh reading, which evidently pushed the film in one direction . . . and I think that Titón was struggling so that the film would become . . . and I think that both the short story and the film have a certain restraint and that has made it a rather uncomfortable film for the more rigid structures in the country; because it is unsettling, it is disturbing, but then you think that it isn't, because you feel it's made by someone who really wants to understand, just like the story.

27

SP: There's also the fact that during the whole process of making the film the danger of going too far was always there. What I was talking about before, the need all we Cubans have to make political statements, to make a political allegory, was always present. I think that above all we were making a work of art, a film, and that the film wasn't a political act. The film can have all the political significance you want, but first and foremost we were creating a work of art.

RC: The film faced difficult moments when the actors were being selected. Titón had been through that experience and knew about that kind of mistake and he started off with the wrong David.

SP: That's right, Vladimir wasn't going to play the role of David.

RC: He started out with a David who was the right age, and really very handsome but he was pretentious and didn't fit the requirements of the film.

SP: I'd always thought of David as a role for Vladimir and as I wrote the script, I wrote with Vladimir in mind. His physical traits . . . I like to suggest actors to a director, but only suggest, because the selection of actors is a very complex, professional business. But I thought that in the first place Vladimir was a talented actor and physically I felt he was right for the part as a young man uniting that beauty with a particular state of mind. He was someone whose charm might pass unnoticed but Diego would be charmed; I mean Diego would see his beauty, at a level that's much more interesting than that of a magazine model.

Vladimir was working in the interior of the island, when the Special Period was at its harshest, and he was really skinny, and you see that in the film. There are times when he looks as if he's come from a concentration camp. He's very thin but he's also a youth with a very striking face.

And then there was Nancy, the role I wrote for Mirta Ibarra. Ever since the previous film, I'd known how she speaks, her tone of voice, pauses, gestures, I felt her vitality within me and that's very good for a writer. But I wasn't thinking of anyone in particular when I created Diego, of any actor I mean. Sometimes I thought of various people, friends of mine, that would change this scene, or that dialogue when I had someone in mind, he walks like somebody else, he's a synthesis of many different observations. But that wasn't the case with David that I had worked on specifically for Vladimir. When you're writing you can choose an actor for your role even if he's dead! Then the director makes the final decision. But anyway, there were these great expectations for the film. It was really incredible. The film was the main topic of conversation until the raft people started. They replaced us: everyone was suddenly talking about the raft people.

The film is a manifestation of the Special Period, a film made for the Special Period. It's there in the script. A film that doesn't cost anything to make. That was the first comment from the producer, when I thought he would say something about the politics, the ideological content, that kind of worry; the producer said it was the best of all the scripts he had read, because it didn't need petrol. There's no movement, very few exteriors, everything's filmed in one house, nobody goes more than five kilometres – there are three cars – in the whole film. It is a film written to be very cheap to make.

PB: How did the gay community in Cuba react to the film?

SP: In general terms, very positively, and very pleased, in general terms. Some people didn't like it. Not very many

29

reacted that way. Then others thought I was wrong to let the story be turned into a film. They prefer the story to the film. I find that difficult to judge: sometimes they'd say they like the film but prefer the story. As far as I'm concerned, they're both mine; I'm not upset by either attitude because I'm pleased they like them both.

PB: Do they dislike the role of Nancy?

SP: Some gays say that they don't like the character of Nancy, and it seems they're upset by the fact that there's no relationship between Diego and David; they say that's a limitation, it's a cowardly avoidance of a wholly homosexual affair; and some people are upset by Diego's mannerisms in some scenes.

PB: Some gay critics have criticised the structure of the film, saying that a bourgeois melodrama is not a suitable frame for dealing with gay questions, that there is no sense of erotic enjoyment, that Diego is a racist . . .

SP: Yes, I know people make these criticisms. They concentrate on this level rather than the political one. They resist the film. Look, there's been this criticism of Diego in the gay world, that he's too camp, that it's an out-of-date image of homosexuals . . . that homosexuals act normally in society. And I would say it is one of the great gains of the gay movement that the homosexual is accepted as not necessarily being this caricature that has always been a butt, a clown, flouncing around, undermining the seriousness of the discourse . . .

PB: Because Diego is a queen.

SP: That's right and then there is the stereotyped image of the homosexual, the laughing-stock who has justified all the laughs and has damaged the gay movement. We had these doubts when we were making the film. There were two options open to us, either Diego would be camp or he wouldn't. We always made this film with Cuba in mind and never thought it would make an impact elsewhere. Within the Cuban context the homosexuals who have really suffered and been repressed are queens, the ones who have a public presence. I think a queen has a right to appear in public. There's no reason why it should all be bottled up inside. In fact, I think there is some prejudice within the gay movement itself against gays who act like this. They find them embarrassing. But this mannered behaviour was not an invention of the film, it's there in reality. In the Cuban context, the homosexual who remains in the closet, the one I mention in my story, who's got a moustache, smokes, and probably has two children and four wives, though he's essentially homosexual, has never had any problems at all. He doesn't suffer. The homosexual who acts like a heterosexual isn't the one who really suffers. If you're involved in the world of art and culture, you might a bit, because if you're an artist you're immediately suspected of being homosexual even if you're not. That's why we opted for the visible homosexual, the one everyone laughs at, the one everyone holds in contempt. Because in our culture there are lots of double standards about. For various reasons, somebody might be judged to be homosexual, but because he doesn't seem that way, everybody goes along with him, everybody is in the know but nobody says a word. So there are members of the Party, where nobody must ever find out, and everyone overlooks details that might raise suspicions. There are people who . . . because of the way they feel they have to act . . . who may be homosexuals, but there's no

31

proof, there's no evidence; and then suddenly they're people with problems, who've been found out, and they are completely crushed.

With these double standards it's very easy to carry on in societies like ours. But not if you're camp . . . Nobody can take you seriously, give you work . . . You can't compare Cuba to England and other countries in Europe; the tradition here is much more *machista*, there's much more rigid intolerance, although I do think that in questions of sexuality and homosexuality greater understanding is developing, but we haven't yet reached your level of development. I mean, things which in England are gains, don't exist here. First there were gay bars, clubs and publications in Europe; I'm sure that in Mexico, in Paraguay, in Venezuela, advances are being made, but these issues haven't been resolved. That's why we decided on a camp homosexual, and to emphasise his campness which then gradually fades in the course of the film. For that's also my personal experience, you meet a homosexual with all these camp gestures and you're shocked because you don't know who he is; all your prejudices come together, he's frivolous and promiscuous, the whole sorry story, and, sometimes, when you get to know him, he's a charming human being, full of moral values, and then you no longer see the mannerisms that once upset you, you take them on board, you don't see them any more and they no longer irritate you.

PB: There has been repression in Cuba . . .

SP: Diego says it very clearly in the film: in Cuba there have been evident homophobia and double standards; people have gone along with this and it's had a political side, particularly in relation to intellectuals. It was always going to be easier to repress someone's ideas if that someone was homosexual, because he could rely on help from no quarter. In our tradition, nobody showed solidarity with homosexuals for fear of being stigmatised as homosexual. And so they let them stew in their own juice. And in this sense – Diego says this very clearly – many homosexuals emphasise their homosexuality and gestures, in order to be seen as clowns and buffoons, because to a certain extent as a clown you become unimportant, and people stop worrying about you and let you get on with life. They reject you but think you're unimportant. It's a kind of self-defence if you like, the option to exaggerate your homosexuality. We're also talking here of something in the past. Things have changed. Some things have been resolved and others are more difficult.

There's also been discrimination within the homosexual community. One part of the gay world was pleased to see itself represented in the film by a person who is normal, more or less male and integrated within society. There has been a rejection of the marginalised gay, the very camp, the very effeminate, transvestites, people really screwed up by what's happened to them, the old, the ugly and the promiscuous. In Cuba there have been lots of rejections: gay blacks, for aesthetic rather than racial reasons, and old gays. I often hear people say homosexuality is about youth and beauty. And there's a lot of racism. I've heard people talking about a Mexican gay magazine where the gays are Indian and they think it's a joke. People want to see themselves represented by beautiful well-educated gays, not by the black sheep. I think this often happens with minorities and it's very understandable. There's an aggression which comes from being on the defensive. The black who wants to identify with the intellectual and rejects the sensual figure of the dancer . . . It happens with all marginalised people. I don't know what it's like in Europe but it's very Latin American. People are more interested in the reflection of reality than in reality itself. The ugly and the dirty should be consigned to the kitchen and what's attractive kept for the living room.

The other consideration is that it is a film made in the Caribbean where physical expression is very important. You walk down the street, and you can't tell the homosexual from the non-homosexual: there are much more openly erotic gestures from people walking down the street than ever you'll get in Europe . . .

PB: There has been criticism of the lack of homo-erotic love in the film?

SP: I swear that I've no problem with writing a story about love between two men. Woody Allen wrote a story about being in love with a sheep. There's a psychiatrist and a patient in love with a sheep. The psychiatrist tries to take away the sheep. You have to admit that the sheep played by Raquel Welch is very attractive! I've got no problems about writing any kind of love story. But the story that came to me, in the context in which I was writing, was not about love between two men. If I had turned it that way, I think it would have impoverished and limited the story. It would have been important but it wouldn't have got beyond the theme of gayness and wouldn't have developed into other areas.

There was something to do that was more difficult and complex, much more necessary, in the Cuban situation. Here there has been a development during the Eighties in relation to homosexuality – from the point of view of censorship. There have been mistakes and excesses caused by homophobia in Cuban society. Perhaps the story and the film will help finish off that process. The spiritual conditions existed where that past could be confronted. Some things had been overcome but it was important from my point of view to analyse this history, and its human and social meaning. To go beyond the issue of homosexuality. For me the acceptance of diversity within human behaviour including sexuality is a much broader theme, and much richer and more complex than merely a gay story. I think it's more interesting and it's quite obvious this film is relating a story about a gay but that it's not a gay film because the theme is not gayness . . . It's something else. It's a film which is aimed at heterosexuals. It is heterosexuals who have to be educated. Heterosexuals have to understand how inhuman, how barbaric it is to deny the possibility of the existence of other forms of expression, of relationships. In that sense, the film is about accepting diversity, accepting difference, and different behaviour in life, in the terrain of homosexuality and in other terrains. I reckon it's important that it is the story of the relationship between a homosexual and a heterosexual. I think it's important that heterosexuals respect homosexuals and vice versa and that they can live together. In Cuba we don't yet have what exists in Europe where homosexuals live in ghettoes and there are bars for homosexuals, theatres for homosexuals, cinemas for homosexuals. I think that the ideal should be that everything should be for everybody, that we should share, not separate out. Some shouldn't go one way and others another. They are artificial divisions!

In this sense I felt the need to make the central theme of the film the apprenticeship of tolerance, that David should learn to tolerate people who are not the same as himself in their sexuality or in other aspects of their lives. That's essential in the Cuban context. And what's more to understand that this country and this society are made up of people you like and people you don't like. People of one sort and another. It's very important to say these things in Cuba. This country is apparently only heterosexual, atheist and socialist. If one isn't sexually heterosexual, politically Marxist-Leninist and spiritually atheist, then you can't be Cuban. In the film and the story what we're saying is that this restricts and impoverishes life. Lots of people don't fit in those categories, and they have an equal right to form part of this society with those who do display the canonical virtues that are based on a dogma. This is the meaning of the film. So within the restrictions imposed by the genre, I had to establish that it was about two people and two different sexual options: one homosexual and one heterosexual. That's one of the reasons I introduce the character of Nancy, apart from simply dramatic reasons. I need things to happen to David and to Diego. I need an interlocutor for David. I wrote one version where it was Germán, the other homosexual, but that tilted the film towards homosexuals and the gay issue . . .

Just to make sure that this is clear in relation to the theme of the film. There are two different kinds of people and the problem lies in their accepting and understanding each other, in their discovering each other. It's very important dramatically to establish that David isn't homosexual because if David were homosexual then his understanding of Diego has less merit because it becomes an act of solidarity, it would have been a process of identifying with him, of removing a burden he suffers because of their homosexuality. My version of the relationship is more complex – I accept you although I'm not like you, I accept your worth and it is equal to mine.

Then there is the character of Nancy. She's played by Mirta who is married to Titón. Lots of people have said she was put in by the director. That's not true at all. I saw Mirta, talked to her, and created the role. I was exploring the possibility of a third main character. I was going to make that Germán but then decided not to and stuck with the character of Nancy.

PB: What about the comment that the film is seen from David's perspective?

SP: That's quite true. It is shot from the point of view of the heterosexual. But I think the intention has been misunderstood. I wanted to concentrate on David's apprenticeship, the apprenticeship of an atheistic, socialist heterosexual in the understanding of everything outside this schema, who develops and at the end of the film has a friend who is homosexual and religious, and is now open to the other side of Cuban reality.

I think one of the main problems in this country, in this nation, is the need to understand the diversity of behaviour among Cubans and to accept this diversity not as a tragedy but as something enriching.

In a very conscious way Diego is a character who enriches David's life in a definitive manner, makes him lead a fuller life, become a better human being. The problem has to be seen in the Cuban context. David is also a member of the Young Communists, he's very committed, he defends the Revolution, and has a concept of the Revolution; as he says at one point, if the Revolution doesn't understand and come to terms with these things, it isn't the Revolution. The Revolution has to be something where homosexuals, religious believers, people who are different, can live openly, and this cannot happen in a dogmatic, intolerant atmosphere as has existed within the Revolution. The Revolution has had within it characteristics which negate it.

PB: There's also the bisexual option . . .

SP: Another issue with the film is that it is a film. It's telling a story and is not a congress to debate homosexuality and society in Cuba!

PB: It's said that a film about homosexuality should be written and directed by homosexuals . . .

SP: People have to understand what the film is trying to do. There have been lots of criticisms of this kind. The film was made in the Cuban context and it was important to have a film that centred seriously on homosexuality, that operated with a greater level of freedom than has been possible and which developed thinking among heterosexuals. To have raised more gay issues and bisexuality would have put the emphasis much more on the gay terrain where I think the argument has been won. Here, convincing heterosexuals of the rights of homosexuals is a necessary operation. I think that one of the main values of the film is that it establishes a dialogue between different parts of society and different positions and doesn't do so stridently. As Titón has said, the film isn't proselytising on behalf of homosexuality but engaging in a conversation with heterosexuals and defending the rights of homosexuals. One has to say that there are also some very sectarian views in the gay world.

THE WOLF, THE WOODS
AND THE NEW MAN
BY SENEL PAZ
Translated by PETER BUSH

Ismael and I left the bar, said goodbye, sorry David, but it's two o'clock already, and I was left feeling I wanted to chat and not be by myself. I thought I'd go to the cinema then decided not to, just as I got to the ticket office, I wondered about phoning Vivian, then decided not to, thinking to myself: well, David, the best thing would be to wait for the bus to Coppelia, the Ice-Cream Palace. And then . . . well, Diego.

The Ice-Cream Palace, that's what a queer friend of mine called the place. I call him a queer with affection and because he wouldn't want to be called anything else. His theory went like this. 'Homosexual is when you like them up to a point and you can control yourself,' he'd say, 'as well as the ones whose social (I mean, political) position is so inhibiting it makes prunes out of them.' I could almost be listening to him now, standing in the doorway to his balcony, holding a cup of tea. 'But real queers are like me, David, we lose our cool at the mere hint of a phallus, we go wild, in fact. Queers with a capital Q, and there's no two ways about it.'

We met right here at the Coppelia, on one of those days when you've finished your bite to eat and can't decide where to take a stroll. He came over to my table, mumbled 'scuse me' and sat down in the chair opposite with his bags, briefcase, umbrella, bundles of paper and helping of ice-cream. I glanced at him: you didn't have to be a genius to see which way the wind blew; there was chocolate on the menu, he'd ordered strawberry. We were in one of the more central areas of the ice-cream parlour, which was in turn very close to the university, so that at any moment one of my friends might see us. Then they'd ask me who my lady friend in the Coppelia was, and why didn't I bring her to the Residence and introduce her.

Just a tease, nothing malicious, but as I always put up a poor defence or get jittery when I'm innocent, a leg pull

41

would lead to suspicions, and then they'd add, David's a bit of a mystery, David watches what he says, has anyone ever heard him say 'Fuck me, that's shit-easy'? Has David had a girl friend since Vivian left him, and why do you think she left him? The sensible option would be to head out of the ice-cream parlour at top speed in whatever direction. But at that time I didn't make the sensible choices I once did, when I almost made a real mess of my life by always choosing ever so sensibly . . . It felt as if a cow was licking my face. It was the newcomer's lecherous look, I knew it, these people are like that, my stomach just seized up. In the countryside such fruitcakes are defenceless, they're a laughing-stock and try not to be seen in public; but I'd heard that they're something else in Havana, that they set their own rules. And if the next time he looked at me, I gave him a clout, knocked him to the floor and he sicked up his strawberry ice-cream, he'd shout at me, loud enough for everyone to hear: 'Hey, dearie, why did you do that? I swear I wasn't looking at anyone else, darling.' He could lick as much as he liked, he wouldn't provoke me. And when he realised the tricksy stuff wouldn't deliver, he placed another bundle on the table. I smiled to myself because I realised it was bait, and no way was I prepared to bite. I just looked at him out of the corner of my eye, and saw they were books, foreign editions, and the one right on top I could make out, because it was on top: 'Seix Barral, Biblioteca Breve, Mario Vargas Llosa, *La guerra del fin del mundo*.' Amazing! He had that book! Vargas Llosa was a reactionary who poured shit on Cuba and Socialism wherever he went, but I was desperate to read his latest novel and there it was: queers get to everything first. 'Scuse me while I put this lot away,' he said as he tucked the books away in a bag with incredibly long straps that hung down from his neck. 'Fuck him,' I thought, 'the fellow's got more pouches than a kangaroo.' 'I've got more pouches than a kangaroo,' he said with a smirk. 'This stuff is too lethal for public display. We've got a cultured police-force. But if you're interested, I'll show you them . . . somewhere else.' I swapped my red membership card of the Union of Communist Youth from one pocket to another, so that he could see my tastes as a reader implied no intimate bond between us – or did he really want me to call one of his cultured policemen? He didn't get the message at all. He smirked at me again and concentrated on getting a drop of ice-cream on the tip of his spoon which he then lifted onto the tip of his tongue: 'It's delicious, isn't it? The only thing they do properly in this country. Soon it'll be for export only, and we'll be on sugared water.' Why put up with this from a queer? I filled my mouth with ice-cream and began masticating. He was quiet for a moment. 'I know you really well. I've often seen you walking round here with a newspaper under your arm. Little innocent, how do you like calle Galiano?' I made no response. 'A friend of mine who doesn't at all look the part, and knows you as well, saw you in a provincial meeting of some committee or other and told me you were from Las Villas like Carlos Loveira.' He gave a whimper of delight: he'd discovered an almost whole strawberry in his ice-cream. 'Today's my lucky day, I keep finding tasty morsels.' Again I made no response. 'Whatever they say about people from Oriente and Havana, you people from Las Villas are proud to be from Las Villas, and that's really ridiculous.' He was struggling to get the strawberry on his spoon but the strawberry didn't want to go. I'd finished my ice-cream and couldn't think how to leave because that's another of my problems: I can't begin or finish a conversation, I listen to everything people want to tell me though I'm not the least interested. 'Are you keen on Vargas Llosa, Young Communist comrade?' he asked poking the strawberry with his finger. 'Would you read him? They'll never publish his works here. Goytisolo sent me the one you just saw from Spain, it's his latest.' He sat and stared at me. I started to count: when I reached fifty I would stand up and get the hell out of here. He let me reach thirty-nine. He lifted his spoon to his mouth and, savouring his strategy more than his strawberry, said: 'Look, if you come home with me and let me flick open your fly buttons one by one, I'll lend it you – *Thorvald*.'

If he'd known the effect his words would have on me, Diego would have avoided that shaft. He touched a nerve which should be left well alone. Blood rushed to my head, the veins in my neck swelled up, I felt dizzy and my vision clouded over. Four years earlier, my sixth-form literature teacher, a frustrated theatre director as well as a frustrated literature teacher, got the chance of a lifetime when our school didn't reach first place in the inter-school championships because its cultural activities didn't rate. She went to see the Principal and persuaded him, first, that Rita and I were oozing histrionic talent, and second, that she could give us firm direction in *A Doll's House*, a play that might be foreign, comrade Principal, but as Martí said, bring the world into our Republic, and it was ideologically sound and appeared in the programme of studies as revised by the Ministry last summer. The Principal was delighted to accept (it was his chance of a lifetime), and Rita, well, just imagine: stage fright prevented her from answering the class register when it was called, but she harboured this mad passion for me. For my part, I gave a resounding no. My concept of manliness was too elevated to let me get into acting, or rather my friends' was. The Principal didn't mince his words: it was a task, Alvarez David, a task set by the Revolution, thanks to which you, the son of poverty-stricken peasants, have been able to study; the main scenario now in the struggle against imperialism is not, I can tell you, a drama in some theatre; it is in those Latin American countries where

44

young people of your age face daily repression, whilst all we ask of you is something as straightforward as playing a character from Ibsen. I accepted. And not because I had no choice. He persuaded me. He was right. I learned my role and Rita's within a week, because she took her secret passion for me so seriously that she clammed up whenever I went near her. She was yet another of those pallid, defenceless, ugly and usually orphaned girls that keep falling in love with me, and whose boyfriend I generally end up out of a sense of pity and because I don't like to see people with hang-ups. The night of the one and only performance, the night when Diego discovered and pigeon-holed me forever, her stage fright was compounded by nervousness before an audience, nervousness before the jury and the worst, most damning nervousness of all because it would be her last time in my arms, that is, the arms of that nineteenth-century individual I performed in a costume designed by our literature teacher. And right near the end she could help herself no more and stood speechless in the middle of the stage, eyeing me like a sheep's head on a butcher's slab. Our teacher began to choke, the Principal broke a tooth and the audience closed their eyes. As the actor under instructions, I didn't get flustered at this moment of great difficulty for the Fatherland and the Theatre. 'You look worried but say nothing, Nora,' I said as I walked slowly towards her hoping to step on her foot or kick her in the rear. 'I know. We must talk. Should I sit down? It will take time.' But it was hopeless, Rita was too far gone and the play had to continue as Thorvald's self-critical monologue until the literature teacher reacted, had two screens lowered and to the tune of *Swan Lake*, the only music available in the projection room, began showing slides of women workers and militia, of quotations from the First Congress on Education and Culture and poems by stalwarts Juana de Ibarbourou, Mirta Aguirre, and her very own, and, as a

45

result, she later claimed, the play acquired a relevance and depth that Ibsen's play always lacked. 'I have never in my life been so embarrassed,' Diego confessed to me later. 'There was nowhere to hide in my seat, half the audience was praying for you and there was even talk of engineering a black-out. Besides, in the red and green plaid jacket and black baggy trousers you looked as if you were disguised in an African flag. We were moved by your sang-froid, and the innocent way you played the fool. That's why we applauded so enthusiastically.' That was the worst bit, the pitying tone of their applause. As I listened to them, under the spotlights, I prayed fervently that collective amnesia would descend on everyone present and that never, *jamais de la vie*, listening God? should I meet up with any of them, anyone who might recognise me. On the other hand, I pledged to think twice when they next assigned me a task, to stop masturbating, and to take a scientific, technological degree, because that's what the country needed. And I kept to that, except for the scientific-technological bit, and as far as masturbating went, God had to understood it was all down to despair and lack of experience; but He, for his part, failed me: he forgot his word and sent me into Coppelia on a day when I wasn't even feeling clear-headed, and sat me opposite a character who thought he could bribe me because he'd seen me in that state.

'OK, OK, I was only joking,' Diego took fright when he saw me on the verge of a heart attack. 'Forgive me, I was just pulling your leg, so we could relax. Here, have a drink of water. Do you want to go to Out-Patients at the Calixto?' 'No!' I shouted as I stood up and made a decisive move. 'Let's go to your place, look at your books, chat about whatever, why all the fuss?' My nerves were reacting. He looked at me, taken aback. 'Get your things together!' But it was one thing to unload his packages and quite another to pick them up, and while he was doing that he had time to recover. 'But first let me make one or two things clear because I don't want you then saying you were under some misapprehension. You're one of those people whose innocence can be dangerous. Listen to this. One: I'm a queer. Two: I'm religious. Three: I've had my problems with the system; they don't think that I belong in this country, but I'll have none of that, I was born here; first and foremost I'm a patriot and a Lezama Liman, and I'm not leaving here even if they torch my arse. Four: I was imprisoned during the UMAP round-ups. And five: my neigbours spy on me, scrutinise every visitor. Do you still want to come?' 'Yes,' said the son of poverty-stricken peasants, in a hoarse voice I could hardly recognise.

His flat, henceforth to be called the Den, since it was usual for solitary dwellers in Havana to baptise their tiny homes – by now you'd been to the Drawer, the Closet, the Asteroid, the Alternative, All Give and No Take – comprised a room with a bathroom that had been partly converted into a kitchen. The ceiling, a kilometre above the floor, was decorated in the corners and at the centre with those cow pats which in Havana are called soffits, and, like the walls and the furniture, was painted white, while the decorative detail and woodwork, kitchenware, bedlinen and everything else were in red. White or red, except for Diego, who dressed in shades of black to the lightest grey, with white socks, pink spectacles and a pink handkerchief. That day almost all the space was taken up by wooden saints with faces fit to depress anyone. 'What wonderful carvings,' he exclaimed as we got in, making it clear that this was art and not religion. 'Germán, the sculptor, is a genius. You watch him turn our plastic arts upside down in a way you won't like at all. The cultural attaché from one of the embassies has expressed an interest and yesterday we got a call from the Spanish Press Agency.' I knew little about art, but some time later, when the representative from the Ministry of Culture declared that the message they communicated wasn't at all positive, I thought he wasn't far wrong, and told Diego as much. 'Let them broadcast this on Radio Nacional!' he bellowed. 'This is art. And that's not for my sake, David. It's for Germán. The moment the news reaches Santiago de Cuba, the place will explode. They'll probably give him the sack.'

But the problems over Germán's exhibition were to come later. Now I'm in the centre of his Den, surrounded by saints with stomach ache and certain I've come to the wrong place. As soon as I could get the book, I'd be on my way. 'Take a seat,' he said, 'I'll make you a cup of tea to calm you down.' He went to close the door. 'No!' I snarled. 'As you like, make it easy for the neighbours. Sit in that arm- chair. It's special, I don't offer it to everybody.' He went into the bathroom, and I heard his voice above the spurt of urine: 'I use it exclusively to read John Donne and Cavafy, although Cavafy is an indulgence of mine. He should be read in a Viennese chair or astride an unfinished wall.' He reappeared, telling me John Donne was an English poet who was totally unknown over here, and that he was the only owner of a translation which he was for ever circulating among young people. 'The day will come when he'll even be the talk of the Dos Hermanos bar, I can assure you. But, please, do have a seat.' John Donne's armchair sank down till my backside was below my feet, but a quick shuffle and I was perfectly comfortable. 'Shall I put some music on? I've got all sorts. Original recordings of María Melibrán, Teresa Stratas, Renata Tebaldi and Callas, naturally. They're my favourites. Any of them or Celina González. Who would you prefer?' 'I don't know who Celina González is,' I said frankly and Diego doubled up with laughter. People in Havana think you spend your time at peasant dances if you come from inland. 'All right, all right. You've earned the honour of being the first to listen to a record of Callas that I've just received from Florence with her 1955 version of *La Traviata* at La Scala, Milan. Florence in Italy, naturally.' He put the record on and went into the kitchen. 'What's your handle? Mine's Diego. They always joke, Dig you Diego. It's like Anton the Phantom. What's your name?' 'Juan Carlos Rondón, at your service.' He stuck his head out. 'Another liar from Las Villas. You're David. I know everything about everybody. Anybody of interest, that is. You're a writer.' When he brought the tea in he tripped and spilt some milk over me. He wasn't pacified till I agreed to take my shirt off. He washed it in a trice and hung it out on the balcony next to a Spanish shawl that he also brought out of the bathroom. He sat down opposite me, and put a bag of chocolates in my lap. 'At last we can talk in peace. You decide the topic, I don't want to impose myself.' Rather than reply, I lowered my head and stared at a floor-tile. 'Can't you think of anything? Very well then, I'll tell you how I became a queer.'

It happened when he was twelve and a boarder in a school run by priests. One afternoon, he couldn't remember why, he needed to light a candle and as he couldn't find a match, he went to the senior pupils' dormitory, and as it turned out, went in through their shower area. One of the school basketball players was singing under the shower, his naked body covered in soap suds, 'we're so much in love, must we part?, no more pleading . . .' 'He was red-haired, red curly hair,' he sighed, 'at an age when you're neither fourteen nor fifteen. A stream of light was shining down, more worthy of the rose windows of Notre Dame than the skylight of our Marian Brothers' convent, and lit up his back, giving his foamy body a rainbow hue.' The boy was aroused, he added, was clasping his cock, the inspiration of his serenading, and the fascinated Diego was unable to take his eyes off the other boy, who looked at him and let him return the look. No

49

words were exchanged: the demi-god took him by the arm, spun him against the wall and possessed him. 'I went back to the dormitory with my candle out,' he said, 'but burning within, and thrilled at suddenly understanding the world.' But destiny held a bitter surprise in store. Two days later, when he went for another candle, he discovered that his violator had been killed by a kick to the head: trying to retrieve a football, he got mixed up with the legs of the mule that carted coal to the school, which, insensitive to his charms, had delivered the fatal blow. 'From then on,' Diego concluded as he looked at me, 'my whole life has been about my quest for my ideal basketball player. You've got something of him.'

It was obvious he had perfected the technique of stimulating the interest of recruits and students, and also of putting the uptight at ease, as he later revealed. It was just a question of making us hear or see what we didn't want to hear or see, and that reaped excellent results with Communists, he said. But he got nowhere with me. I'd come, like the others, I'd sat down in his special armchair, as they had, but, like no one else, I'd glued my eyes to the floor-tile and he never managed to prise me away. He'd been tempted to show me the porno magazine which he kept for the more difficult cases, or to toast me from the bottle of Chivas Regal where a few drops of rum always lingered, but he restrained himself, because that wasn't what he expected from me; and at the end of the evening, when he started to feel hungry, he realised he wasn't prepared to share his reserves with me, and that he couldn't think how to bring the visit to a close. He sat there quietly thoughtful. He had greatly desired this encounter, he later confessed, ever since the time he saw me acting the role of Thorvald in the theatre. He'd even dreamed about it and several times had been on the point of accosting me in calle Galiano, because he'd had an intuition about our friendship

50

from the start. But now he was thinking how wet, as I sat there silent and stiff in the middle of his Den and began to think how yet again he had fallen victim to a mirage, to his tendency to bestow sensitivity and talent upon those of us who had that look of butter-wouldn't-melt. He was really surprised and upset he had misjudged me. I was his last card, the last he had to play before he concluded that everything was shit, that God had been mistaken and Karl Marx even more so, that this would-be new man, in whom he placed so much hope, was pure fantasy, a joke, socialist propaganda, because if there was a new man in Havana it couldn't be one of those strapping, handsome special Commandos, but someone like me, ready to play the innocent, one he would bump into some day and entice into his Den, with an offer of tea and conversation; conversation, for fuck's sake, he wasn't always thinking about the same thing, as he later explained to me when pontificating. 'I'm off,' I said in the end, as I stood up; I looked at him, we looked at each other. He spoke without stirring from his chair. 'David, do come back. I don't think I've explained myself today. Perhaps I seemed superficial to you. Like anyone who talks a lot, I talk nonsense. That's because I'm nervous, but I felt different talking to you. Talking is important, a dialogue doubly so. Please don't be afraid to come back. I have my self-respect and can control myself like anyone else and help you a lot, lend you books, get you tickets to the ballet. I'm very close to Alicia Alonso and would like to introduce you one day to the Loynaz household, at five pm, a privilege I alone can bestow. I'd like to offer you a Lezama Lima lunch, something I don't offer everybody. I know that the generosity of queers is double-edged, as Lezama himself notes somewhere in his work, but not in this case. Do you want to know why I like talking to you? Straight from the heart. I think we'll understand each other though we're different. I know there are good things in the

Revolution, but I've had bad experiences, and, besides, I've got my own ideas about some things. Maybe I've got it wrong, it could be. I'd like to discuss things, for people to listen and explain. I'm prepared to reason, to change my mind. But I've never been able to talk to a revolutionary. You only talk to yourselves. You couldn't care less about what the rest of us think. Do come back. I'll put the issue of queers to one side, I promise you. Here, take *The War of the End of the World*, and *Three Trapped Tigers* as well, you won't find that out there either.' 'No!' I said it so forcefully he was frightened. 'Why, David, what's it matter?' 'No!' I repeated slamming the door behind me.

That was well done, I thought when I was out in the street, the bang still echoing in my ears: I neither took his books nor accepted them as presents. My Spirit, which had been agitating inside me the whole time, relaxed and began to feel a degree of pride in this lad, who at the end of the day had come up trumps. That's what it expects of me, a young communist who in meetings always got a word in edgeways and, though falteringly, always said what he thought, whom Bruno had already asked after twice. That's as far as my Spirit goes, but it's not so easy with my Conscience, and before I reached the corner it was demanding a few explanations. Spell it out slowly and clearly, David Alvarez, why, if you were a real man, had you gone to the home of a homosexual; if you were a revolutionary, to the home of a counter-revolutionary, and if you were an atheist, why had you gone to the home of a believer? All this as I walked along, got on the bus, put up with the pushing and shoving. Why had it been possible in your presence to make fun of the Revolution (your Revolution, David), and wax lyrical on a sick, perverse strain without your taking a stand? Didn't your membership card burn a hole in your pocket, or were you just carrying it around for fun? Who are you really, my young lad?

Are you forgetting you're only peasant trash the Revolution dragged out of the mire and brought to study in Havana? But if I've learned one thing in my life, it is not to respond to my Conscience in a crisis situation. On the contrary, I caught it out when I got off in the university, rushed up the steps at top speed, searched out Bruno, took him into a quiet corner and asked him what you do, whom do you inform when you meet someone who receives foreign books, slanders the Revolution and is religious. How about that then, Conscience? Bruno thought the matter so important that he removed his spectacles and took me to see another comrade, and the moment I saw the other comrade I was convinced I was going to put my foot in it again. Like Diego, he had a clear, penetrating gaze, as if that day clear, penetrating gazes were joining forces to fuck me up. He led me into an office, pointed to a chair that was neither Viennese nor anything like and told me to speak out. I told him how we revolutionaries always had to be vigilant, ever on red alert; and it was because I was vigilant and on red alert that I'd met Diego, gone to his house and knew what I now knew about him. Rightaway I'd been suspicious about his foreign books and obscene jibes. Did he understand? Either he didn't understand or the story made no impact on him. He yawned once, even leafed through some papers while pretending he was listening to me. And that's another of my problems: I get upset when someone's bored with the story I'm recounting and then I start to gesticulate and add all manner of detail. 'The fellow's a counter-revolutionary,' I emphasised. 'He's in touch with the cultural attaché from an embassy and interested in influencing young people.' You mean, I expected the comrade to say, that you went to the house of a religious, counter-revolutionary queer because one always has to be on red alert, is that what you're saying? Of course. But he didn't say that. He turned his clear, penetrating gaze on me and a shiver ran

53

down my spine because I thought I could guess what he was going to say: What a pathetic shit-bag you are, kid, a right little opportunist on the make. But no, he didn't say that either. He smiled, spoke to me in a condescending, ironic or affectionate tone, however I wanted to take it: 'Yes, we must always be vigilant. David, isn't it? The enemy acts where he's least expected, David. Find out which embassy he's in touch with, note down what he asks about military manoeuvres and the whereabouts of our leaders and we'll meet up again. That's your task now, now you're a spy. OK?' This is Ismael. We'll be friends one day, get along famously, and one day I'll offer him a Lezaman lunch because he had also had a literature teacher at some point.

I walked down the steps of the university on the big screen: with a military march playing in the background, I raced along as the flag with its solitary star flapped in the sky. When I got to the Residence I had a good, hot bath, lots of hot water washing over me, till I felt the last worries of the day disappear down the plug-hole, and was able to sleep. But I wanted to end the day on a high note, and threw myself down on my bed where I intended to study a while. That was my mistake. From my bed you can see the sea, it was beautiful, calm and deep blue, and the sea has a terrible effect on me. Inside, alongside my Conscience and Spirit, I carry a Counter-conscience that's even more of a bastard, which started to stir, wanted to wake up and ask questions, and for some reason I couldn't keep my Counter-conscience quiet. Just one of its questions can take me to the twenty-fourth floor and fling me into the void. I put the book down and told myself in the bathroom mirror: 'Fuck me, it's shit easy!' And I promised the man looking down on me that I would help him out, that no way would I go back to that fellow's place, nor to any other Diego's, cross my heart, I wouldn't.

I didn't keep my word. And Diego didn't keep his either.

54

'We homosexuals have got other even more interesting categories than the one I explained to you the other day. That is, those properly called *homosexuals* – the term is commonly used because this word, even in the worst of circumstances, contains an element of respect; *queers* – dear me, also commonly used – and *queens*, the lowest category of which are the so-called *drag queens*. This scale depends on the individual's inclination to social duty or queerdom. When the balance tips towards social duty, you're in the presence of a homosexual. There are those – I include myself in this group – for whom sex has a place in life but is not in place of life. Like heroes or political activists, we put Duty before Sex. The cause we're pledged to takes pride of place. In my case, my mission is national Culture, to which I devote the best of my intellect and time. I'm not boasting but my study of nine-teenth-century Cuban women's poetry, my census of fences and grilles in the calles Oficios, Compostela, Sol and Muralla, or my exhaustive collection of maps of the Island from the arrival of Columbus onwards, are essential reading for any study of our country. One day I'll show you my inventory of seventeenth and eighteenth-century buildings, each accom-panied by a sketch of the exterior and main interior areas, vital ingredients in any future restoration project. All this, as well as my archive where the most valuable papers are seven of Lezama's unpublished manuscripts, is the fruit of many a late night, dear boy, as is my comparative study of buggery slang in the Port and Central Park. I mean, if I'm standing on that balcony where the Spanish shawl is now fluttering, pen in hand, revising my text on the sisters Juana and Dulce María Borrero, I won't abandon the task even though I spot a most fetching mulatto from Marianao walking along the pavement, and fondling his balls the minute he sees me. We homosexuals in this category don't waste time on sex, nothing tempts us from our labours. The idea that we are corruptible and devious by nature is totally mistaken and offensive. No, sir, we're as patriotic and firm as the next man. If it's a choice between cock and Cuba, it's Cuba all the time. Given our intellect and the fruits of our toil we deserve a space that we're always denied. Marxists and Christians, take note, will always be crippled till they recognise our place and accept us as allies, since, more commonly than people admit, we usually share the same sensitivities on social issues. *Queers* don't merit a separate explanation, like anything that's neither one thing nor the other: you'll understand them when I define *queens*, who are very easy to conceptualise. They operate the whole time with a phallus embedded in their brain, and only perform for its benefit. Wasting time is their basic character trait. If the time they invested in flirting in public parks and lavatories were devoted to socially useful work, we'd be heading for what you people call Communism and we call Paradise. The most wastrel of all are the so-called *drag queens*. I hate them because they're fatuous and vacuous, and their lack of discretion and tact has turned such simple, necessary acts as varnishing one's toe-nails into acts of social defiance. They provoke and wound popular sensitivities, not so much because of their mannered behaviour as their stupidity, always giggling for no reason and talking about things they don't understand. A black queen is rejected even more wholeheartedly, since we think of the black as a symbol of virility. And if the wretches live in Guanabacoa, Buenavista or towns inland, their life becomes real hell, because people in those places are even more intolerant. This typology can be applied to heterosexuals of both sexes. In the case of men, the lowest rung, the one that corresponds to drag queens and is marked by time-wasting and desire for perpetual fornication, is occupied by the *horny brigade*, who may, let's say, be on their way to post a letter, when they give one of us a tickle, without undermining their virility, just because they can't keep it down. With women the base-line is occupied by whores of course, but not the ones hovering around the hotels in pursuit of tourists, or any others that just do it for money, of whom we have few examples, as official propaganda points out quite correctly, but those who simply do it for the pleasure; as the plebs rightly say, they like spilt milk. Well now, we have queens, slags and the horny brigade in this paradise under the stars, and when I say that I'm only subscribing to what one English writer said on the subject: 'one can't take out the unpleasant things of this world by simply looking in the other direction.'

And so, with this and other topics of conversation, we became friends, got used to spending the afternoon together, drinking tea from the cups which he said were so valuable, and Sunday lunchtimes became sacred occasions for which we reserved our most interesting discussions. I walked barefoot in his Den, took off my shirt and opened the fridge when I felt like it, an act which the shy provincial would see as the supreme expression of trust and informality. Diego asked to read what I wrote, and when I finally dared to hand him a text, he made me wait a fortnight before passing any comment, then at last he laid it on the table. 'I'll be frank. Prepare yourself: it's no good. Why do you write *muzhik* instead of peasant? You've been reading too many books published by the Revolutionary Press and Progress Books. We'll have to start all over again, because you're not without talent.' And he took my education in hand. 'Read this,' he'd say, handing over the book *Sugar and Society in the Caribbean*, which I'd read. 'Read *Exploring Popular Humour*,' which I'd read. 'Read *Literary Mannerism in America and Cuba*', which I'd read. 'Read *Cuban Counterpoint: Tobacco and Sugar*', which I'd read. 'Put a cover from the army magazine over this and don't leave it around: it's *El monte*, the Afro Bible, OK? And as for poetry, here's *Cuban Poetry*,

57

and something that's gold dust: a complete run of the magazine *Orígenes*, the like of which not even Rodríguez-Feo possesses. You can take that home one at a time. And here we have, but this is definitely for later, everything we do is only preparation to reach this far, the Master's Work, Lezama's complete poetry and prose. Here, put your hand on it, caress it, absorb its sap. One day, one afternoon in November, when the light of Havana is at its most beautiful, we'll walk past his house in the calle Trocadero. We'll come from Prado, on the opposite pavement, chatting affably. You'll wear something blue, a colour that really suits you, and we'll imagine the Master is alive, and that very moment peering through the shutters. Smell the smoke of his cigar, listen to his wheezy breathing. He'll say: "Look at that queen and her young attendant, what an effort to make him, rather than just slipping him a decent ten peso note." No, don't be insulted, he's like that. I know he'll appreciate my effort and recognise your sensitivity and intellect, and though he was often misunderstood, he'll be particularly heartened by your revolutionary status. On that day he'll be happier to read part of his work for half an hour to the bureaucrats from the Council for Culture assigned to the realm of Persephone, a fairly spacious auditorium, to be sure.' On maps spread out on the floor, we found the most delightful buildings and squares of Old Havana, the stained glass which just had to be seen, the best wrought iron work, the columns mentioned by Carpentier, and stretches of three-hundred-year-old wall. He drew up a precise itinerary for me which I followed to the letter, and I came back all excited to comment on what I'd seen in the intimacy of his flat, behind a bolted and barred door, while we drank iced cider, prú oriental or chirimoya shakes, and listened to Saumell, Lecuona, the trio Matamoros or, down low, because of the neighbours, Celia Cruz and the Sonora Matancera. As for ballet, which was his strong point,

I didn't miss a performance. He always got me tickets, however difficult that proved, and when it was really critical, he would give me his invitation. At the theatre we didn't say hello even though our paths crossed on the way in or out, we pretended not to see each other, and his seat was never near mine. To avoid meeting him, I stayed in the auditorium during the intervals, counting the vowels in the programme notes. 'What most surprises me about our friendship,' he would say, 'is that I know as much about you now as I did at the start. Come on, tell me something about yourself, my dear. Your first sexual experience, what age you began to come, what your erotic dreams are like. Don't try to keep me out: with those eyes, you must be pure fire, when you get going. And why?' – he returned to the attack as soon as I tensed up – 'now we're like brothers, won't you let me see you naked? I can tell you, I can never remember the face of a man whose willy I've never seen. Anyway, I can imagine yours as soft as a baby dove; though, I must admit, there are lads who are all sensitive and spiritual like you yet, when they strip off, they stick out one hell of a tool.'

For the Lezama Lima lunch he made me wear a shirt and tie. Bruno lent me one, and forced ten pesos on me as well, thinking that I was taking a girl out to the Tropicana. The exceptional quality of a lunch, as I later discovered Lezama himself wrote in *Paradiso*, springs from its embroidered table-cloth that isn't red or white but cream to contrast with the gleaming white enamel of the dinner service edged in tawny green. Diego took the lid off the soup tureen, where a thick plantain soup was steaming. 'I wanted to rejuvenate you,' he said smiling mysteriously, 'by taking you back to your early childhood, so that's why I've added a little tapioca to the soup . . . ' 'And what's that?' 'Yucca, my baby, but don't interrupt me. I've floated some sweet corn on top, there are just so many things we liked as kids that we've never enjoyed since. But don't worry, it's not the so-called Wild West soup, for whenever some gourmets see sweet corn, they think they can see covered waggons rolling on to California through Sioux Indian territory. And now I must look at my boy's table,' he interrupted his strange patter, which I greeted with a foolish giggle, as I pretended to play along with him. 'Let's change places,' he said collecting up the dishes after we'd finished the terrific soup, ' "canary glitter after graceless prawns: then the second course made its entry as a well-beaten sea-food soufflé, bedecked by a quadrille of prawns, a double chorus line of pincers wafting around the steam rising from pastry packed like white coral. The soufflé also contained the celebrated swordfish and lobsters gawping in livid panic as if their carapaces were greeting the torch that burnt out their bulging eyes." ' I couldn't find words to praise the soufflé, and this shortfall of mine or of my language, turned out to be the best praise of all. ' "After a dish that so successfully preened its strident colours, a flaming Gothic of almost Baroque proportion yet retaining the Gothic in the texture of the dough and the allegories sketched by the prawns, let some light relief into the lunch with this beetroot salad, mayonnaise dressing, Lübeck asparagus"; and keep with us, Juan Carlos Rondŏn, because we're reaching the climax to the ceremony.' And when he went to skewer some beetroot, the whole slice came away and fell on the table-cloth. He couldn't hide his annoyance, and tried to right his error of judgement, but the beet bled again, and at the third attempt the beet fell to pieces where he'd skewered it: one half was left on the fork, and the other slid back on the table-cloth, making three purple islands around the rosettes. I was about to express my dismay, when he gave me an entranced look: 'Such perfection,' he said, 'those three stains make a really splendid setting for our meal.' He continued, almost declamatory: 'In that light, with the stubborn patience of an

60

artisan, the threads ominously channel the vegetable blood, and the three stains arouse dark expectations.' He smiled, delighted in revealing his secret to me: 'You are present at the family lunch that doña Augusta regales in the pages of *Paradiso*, chapter seven. Now you can say you've eaten like a real Cuban, and joined once and for all the brotherhood of the Master's admirers, though you're still unfamiliar with his work.' Next we ate roast turkey, followed by an equally Lezaman ice cream, the recipe for which he offered me to pass on to my mother. 'Baldovino should now bring on the fruit bowl, but I'll go in her absence. I must apologise for the pears and apples which I've put in place of mangos and guavas, they don't go too badly with the mandarins and grapes. Afterwards, naturally, we'll take coffee on the balcony while I recite you poems by the much maligned Zenea, and we'll give the Havana cigars a miss since neither of us likes them. But first', he added with a sudden wave of inspiration as his eyes lighted on the Spanish shawl, 'a little flamenco' and he regaled me with a dashing *zapateado* which he ended abruptly. 'It's loathsome,' he said flinging the shawl away. 'Perhaps one day you'll forgive me, David.' Just what I was thinking, for suddenly I started to feel uneasy, because though enjoying the lunch I couldn't help some nerve ends remaining raw in that feast, on red alert, spectating, concluding that the lobsters, prawns, Lübeck asparagus and grapes must have been bought in the special shops for diplomats and consequently were proof of his relationship with foreigners, which, in my role as special agent, I should communicate to the comrade who was yet to become my Ismael.

Time went pleasantly by, then one Saturday when I came to tea, Diego only half opened the door. 'You can't come in. I've got somebody with me who doesn't want his face to be seen and I'm having the time of my life. Please come back later.' I went off, but only to the other side of the street, in order to see the face of the man who didn't want to be seen. Diego came down straightaway by himself. I saw how nervously he looked up and down the street, before turning the corner at top speed. I hurried and caught sight of him getting into a diplomatic car half-hidden down an alleyway. I had to crouch behind a pillar because they shot out. Diego in a diplomatic car! A pain seared through my chest. For Christ's sake, it was all true. Bruno was right, and Ismael was wrong when he said you had to consider these cases individually. No. One must always be on the alert: queers are treacherous by nature, it's all down to original sin. As for me, no way would I be two-faced. I could quite cheerfully forget the whole episode: my reaction had been pure class-instinct. But I couldn't cheer up. It was painful. It really hurts when a friend betrays you, hell, it's really painful, not to say very annoying to discover you've been stupid yet again, that someone else had duped you quite so easily. You feel really sick when you have no choice but to admit the hardliners are right and that you're just another sentimental shit-bag taken for a ride by the first comer. I went to the Malecón, and as usual, nature took on the colour of my soul: in a moment the sky became overcast, the noise of thunder got nearer and nearer, and there was a hint of rain in the air. My steps took me straight to the university, in search of Ismael, but I was clear-sighted enough – or whatever, because clear-sightedness doesn't come easily – to realise that I wouldn't survive a third encounter with his clear, penetrating gaze, and I halted in my tracks. The second had come after the Lezaman lunch, when I needed to put my mind to rest before it exploded. 'I was mistaken,' I told him then, 'this fellow's fine, just a poor wretch not worth keeping an eye on.' 'But didn't you say he was a counter-revolutionary?' was his ironic rejoinder. 'Even here we have to recognise that his experience of the Revolution has not been the same as ours. It's difficult to be on the side of someone who's asking you to stop being yourself before he even lets you in. I mean . . .' But I added nothing, I still didn't trust Ismael enough to say what I was thinking. 'He's true to himself, acts according to his own lights. He operates with an inner freedom I wish I had as a militant.' Ismael smiled at me. What distinguished Diego and Ismael's clear, penetrating gazes (to bring your bit to an end, Ismael, because this isn't your story) is the fact that Diego's gaze only points things out to you, and Ismael's demands you start changing them rightaway if they're not to his liking. This is why Ismael was the best of the bunch. He would talk about anything under the sun, and when we said goodbye, he would put his hand on my shoulder and say we shouldn't lose sight of one another. I understood he was freeing me from my duties as a special agent and that our friendship was just beginning. What would he think now when I told him what I'd seen? I returned to Diego's block prepared to wait for as long as was necessary. He came back by taxi in the middle of a downpour. I followed him in before he could close the door. 'So my boyfriend's gone,' he joked. 'Why are you looking like that? Don't tell me you're jealous?' 'I saw you getting in the diplomatic car.' He wasn't expecting that. The colour drained from his cheeks, he slumped into a chair, bowed his head. After a moment he looked up; he'd aged ten years. 'Come on, I'm waiting.' Now we'd have his confessions, regrets, pleas for forgiveness, the name of the counter-revolutionary sect he belonged to and I'd go straight to the police, I'd go to the police. 'I was going to tell you, David, but I didn't want you to find out so soon. I'm leaving.'

The tone with which Diego had said 'I'm leaving' has terrible connotations for us. It means you're departing the country forever, that you're erasing yourself from its memory, and it from yours, and, whether you like it or not, you're agreeing to be labelled a traitor. You agree to that from the start because it comes with the price of the ticket. Once it's in your grasp you won't convince anyone you weren't delighted with your purchase. It's not you, Diego. What would you do far from Havana, from those dirty, warm streets and bustling *habaneros*? What would you do in another city, dear Diego, where Lezama wasn't born and Alicia Alonso doesn't put in a final appearance every weekend? A city without bureaucrats and hardliners to criticise, without a David who is getting to like you? 'It's not because of what you think', he said. 'You know I couldn't care less about the political swings and round-abouts. It's because of Germán's exhibition. You're not very perceptive, you don't know the impact it had. They didn't kick him out of his job, I was the one they kicked out. Germán reached a compromise with them, he's rented a room and is coming to Havana to work in arts and crafts. I recognise I went too far in defending his work, that I was undisciplined and acted like a free agent, took advantage of my position, but so what? Now I've got that on my record, I'll only get work in the fields or on building-sites, and you tell me what I'd do with a brick in my hand, where would I put it? It's only a caution, but who will ever give a job to someone with my looks. I know it's not fair, that the law's on my side and in the end they'd have to admit as much and give me compensation. But what am I going to do? Fight? No way. I'm weak, and there's no place for the weak in your world. On the contrary, you behave as if we didn't exist, as if we were only here to mortify you and reach agreements with the bums in exile. You lead an easy life: you don't suffer an Oedipus complex, you're not tortured by beauty, you didn't have a favourite cat which your father chopped up in front of you so as to make a man of you. It's not impossible to be queer and strong. There are plenty of examples. I know that.

But I'm not one of them. I'm weak, I'm terrified about growing old, I can't wait ten or fifteen years for you to have second thoughts, however confident I am the Revolution will finally change its ways. I'm thirty. At most I've got twenty years of active life left. I want to do things, live, make plans, see myself in the mirror of *Las meninas*, give a lecture on the poetry of Flor and Dulce María Loynaz. Don't I have that right? If I were a good Catholic and believed in another life I wouldn't worry, but your materialism is contagious, that's too many years to wait. This is our life, there is no other. Or at any rate, there's probably only this one. Do you understand? They don't want me here, why mess around, I like the way I am, I want to drop a few pansy petals now and then. Who could that possibly upset, honey, if they're my petals?'

His final days here weren't all sad. Sometimes I found him euphoric, flapping around among parcels and old papers. We drank rum and listened to music. 'Before they come to make an inventory, take this typewriter, the electric stove and tin-opener. Your mum will find it useful. These are my studies on architecture and town-planning: a lot of them, right? Very good, too. If I don't have time, send them anonymously to the City Museum. These are the eye-witness accounts of Federico García Lorca's visit to Cuba. It includes a very detailed itinerary and photographs of places and people with captions written by me. Here's an unidentified black. Keep for yourself the poetry anthology to the river Almendares, add whatever poem you feel like, though the Almendares is in no state for poetry. Look at this photo: me in the Literacy Campaign. And these are family photos. I'll take them all with me. This uncle of mine was really gorgeous, he choked on a stuffed potato. This is me with Mum, what a good-looking woman. Let's see, what else do I want to leave you? You've already taken my papers, haven't you? Send whatever articles you think more digestible to *Revolución y Cultura*, where perhaps someone may appreciate them; choose nineteenth-century topics, they get through more easily. Hand over the rest to the National Library, you know to whom. Don't lose that contact, take him the occasional cigar and don't get upset if he makes a pass at you, that's as far as it will go. I'll also give you my contact at the ballet. And as for these cups, David Alvarez, the ones we've drunk so much tea from, I want to lend them to you. If you ever get an opportunity, send them to me. As I said, they're Sèvres porcelain. But that's not why, they belonged to the Loynaz del Castillo family, and are a present. OK, I'll be frank, I filched them. My records and books have already gone, you've taken what were yours and the ones left are to kid the inventory takers. Get me a poster of Fidel with Camilo, a small Cuban flag, the photo of Martí in Jamaica and Mella wearing a hat; but be quick, they've got to go by diplomatic bag with the photos of Alicia in *Giselle* and my collection of Cuban coins and bank-notes. Do you want the umbrella or the shawl for your mum?' I kept putting everything away quietly, then I'd get hopeful and hand them back: 'Diego, why don't we write to someone. Think who we could try. Or let me go and ask for an appointment with a government official, and you wait outside.' He looked at me sadly and would have none of it. 'Do you know any lawyer, any of that suspect lot who is still around? Or somebody in a high-up position who's a closet queer? You've helped lots of people. I graduate in July, in October I'll be working, I can give you fifty pesos a month.' I shut up when I saw his eyes watering, though he always managed to recover. 'My final piece of advice: choose the clothes you wear carefully. You're no Alain Delon, but you have charm and that air of mystery which can open doors, whatever people say.' I was at a loss for words, looked down and started to reorganise and tie up his parcels. 'No! Don't unwrap that. They're Lezama's unpublished papers. Don't look at me like that. I swear I'll never misuse them. I also swore to you I'd never go and I am leaving, but this is different. I'll never bargain with them or hand them over to anyone who can manipulate them politically. I swear. By my mother, the basketball player, and you as well, so there. If I can brave the storm without using them, I'll send them back to you. Don't look at me like that! Do you think I don't understand my responsibilities? But if I'm in a tight spot, they might get me out of it. You've made me feel guilty. Pour me a drink and go.'

As the date of his departure approached, he languished. He slept badly and lost weight. I spent as much time with him as I could, but he didn't say very much, I think sometimes he couldn't even see me. Curled up in John Donne's armchair with a book of poems and a crucifix, his religiosity had now intensified, he seemed pallid and lifeless. A soft, soothing María Callas lulled him. One day he stared at me really intensely (you're still here, Diego, I'll not forget that look of yours) 'Tell me the truth, David,' he asked, 'do you love me?, has my friendship been of any use?, was I ever disrespectful?, do you think I'm damaging the Revolution?' María Callas stopped singing. 'Ours has been a correct friendship and I'm grateful to you.' He smiled. 'You don't change, do you. I'm not talking about being grateful but of love between friends. Please, don't let's be afraid of words anymore.' That was also what I meant, right? but it's difficult for me, and yes he could be sure of my affection and that, to a certain extent, I was someone else, that I'd changed in the course of our friendship, I was more the person I'd always wanted to be. I added: 'I invite you to lunch tomorrow at the Bunny Rabbit. I'll go early and get in the queue. You only have to get there just before twelve. I'll pay. Or would you rather I came for you and we went together?' 'No, David, that's not necessary. Everything's OK the way it's been.' 'Yes, Diego, I insist. I know what I'm saying.' 'All right, but not the Bunny Rabbit. I'm going vegetarian in Europe.' But if what I wanted, or needed, was to put myself on show with him, if that helped to give me peace of mind or something, all right, he would accept. He came to the restaurant at ten to twelve, as people were crowding around the doorway, under a Japanese parasol, in a rig-out that enabled me to spot him two blocks away. He shouted both my surnames across the street, waving an arm weighed down with bracelets. When he was next to me, he kissed me on the cheek and started describing a divine dress he'd just seen in a shop window which would suit me to a T; to his and my surprise, and the queue's, I defended another style so emphatically it quite eclipsed him, because we shy types do shine when we put ourselves out. Our lunch was a celebration of the efficiency of his technique for unbuttoning Communists. And turning to my literary sensibility, he added other titles to my reading list. 'Don't forget Countess Merlin, start researching her. You and that woman will have an encounter which will be the talk of the town.' We finished up with dessert in Coppelia, and then to his Den for a bottle of Stolichnaya. He was great company until the drink ran out. 'I needed this Russian vodka to say two last things to you. David, I think you're rather lacking in initiative. You should be more determined. Your role should be that of an actor, not a spectator. I can assure you this time you'll play it better than in the *Doll's House*. Don't stop being a revolutionary. You'll ask who am I to tell you that. But I do have my moral code, I told you once I'm a patriot and a Lezama Liman. The Revolution needs people like you, because what the Yankees won't manage, the food, the bureaucracy, their kind of propaganda and arrogance, will put an end to, and only people like you can help prevent that. It won't be easy, I can tell you, you'll need lots of courage. The other thing I have to tell you, let's see if I can, because it's really embarrassing, give me the last drop of vodka, that's right: do you remember when we met in Coppelia? That day I gave you a bad time. None of it was chance. I was with Germán, and when we saw you, we laid a bet that I'd bring you to my Den and bed you. It was a bet in foreign currency, I accepted it to get my courage up to take you on, since you had always inspired a respect I found paralysing. When I spilt the milk over you, it was part of the plan. Your shirt next to the Spanish shawl, draped over the balcony, were the symbols of my victory. Naturally, Germán has spread it around, and more so now he hates me. In some circles, because of late I've been seen only with you, they call me the Red Queen, and others think that my departure is only a pretext, that really I'm a spy with a mission in the West. Don't get too upset, for if such doubts exist about a man, they're not damaging, they make him mysterious and lots of women fall into his arms attracted by the idea of bringing him back to the right path. Will you forgive me?' I said nothing, which he interpreted positively, that I did forgive him. 'You see, I'm not the angel you thought I was. Could you have done such a thing behind my back?' We looked at each other. 'All right, I will make a last cup of tea. Then you must go and not come back. I don't want any goodbyes.' And that was that. When I got out in the street, a line of Pioneers blocked my way. They were wearing freshly ironed uniforms and carrying bunches of flowers; and although a Pioneer with a bunch of flowers had for ages been a tired emblem of the future, inseparable from slogans exhorting us to struggle for a better world, I liked them, perhaps because of that, and I stared at one of them, who stuck his tongue out when he noticed me; and then I told him (I told, didn't promise) that I would defend the next Diego to cross my path tooth and nail, though nobody would understand me, and that wouldn't distance me from my Spirit and Conscience; quite the contrary, if you thought about it, it

69

would be fighting for a better world for you, Pioneer, and for myself. And I wanted to bring the chapter to a close by finding a way to thank Diego for all he had done for me, and I did so by coming to Coppelia and asking for this particular ice-cream. Because there was chocolate on the menu but I'd ordered strawberry.

STRAWBERRY AND CHOCOLATE
A Screenplay by
SENEL PAZ
Translated by Peter Bush

EXPLANATORY NOTE

This is not the 'script of the film', but the script the writer gave the director as the final fruit of his literary endeavours. People have said, and I quite agree, that it is the film that matters, namely the director's interpretation and realisation of the script. A film is also a specific experience of filming during which fertile suggestions and solutions arise together with difficulties and obstacles that frustrate previous ideas, all of which transform and shape the definitive work. It is the natural interplay between the original project and the final work that is particularly rich in the art of the cinema. And it is the relationship that exists between the present text (the project) and the film on screen (the work). It is appropriate to point out, together with the other authors of the film, that the variations between film and script, generally few in number, derive from the act of creation and not from any kind of censorship or 'betrayal'.

SENEL PAZ, Havana, 1994.

SYNOPSIS

This is the story of David, a youngster from a peasant background, with a wide range of prejudices, who is studying Political Sciences at the University of Havana in the 1970s. He is a member of the Young Communists and aspires to become a writer. It is the story of his frustrated first love and sexual initiation with a whore who 'officially doesn't exist'. And, above all, it is the story of his friendship with Diego, a homosexual who loves and defends the national culture of Cuba, 'a Lezaman and a patriot' as he defines himself, a man who doesn't understand a Revolution that in turn neither understands nor accepts him. It is also the story of David and Miguel, his political comrade, who holds views of the world that are opposed to his. It is, in brief, a story about friendship, the persistence of dogmas and the pursuit of tolerance.

1. HAVANA. EXT. DAY
Free cinema. Havana, a city in the thrall of machismo, a world with no place for the weak and the effeminate. Lingering shots of masculine gestures and exuberance. Women play a subordinate role, enjoy participating in the virility cult. An affectionate, good-humoured view of the city and its people.

2. THE PALACE OF MATRIMONY: ENTRANCE. EXT. DAY
The bride is late. The bridegroom, relatives and guests wait rather anxiously. A degree of tension. The bridegroom is making an effort to appear calm. His friends crack jokes. The notary indicates he can't wait any longer. A fat woman runs up to say the bride has just arrived. The bridegroom breathes a sigh of relief.

    Radiant, majestic, the world at her feet, the bride (VIVIAN), *resplendent in immaculate white, gets out of the car and, on her father's arm, walks up the steep steps leading to the Palace of Matrimony. She is 20 years old and very beautiful. The bridegroom is 30.*

3. THE PALACE OF MATRIMONY: MAIN ROOM. INT. DAY
The marriage. A traditional, kitsch ceremony. The notary reads extracts from the Family Code. The bridegroom is in a nervous sweat. VIVIAN *is calm personified. Over these images,* DAVID's *voice-over seems like the thoughts of the uneasy bridegroom.*

DAVID's VOICE: The woman in my life . . . Pure and immaculate, till tonight's over with.
    The moment for the forms to be signed. The NOTARY *gives his final instructions. The bridegroom seems more and more unsure. The* NOTARY *offers his pen to* VIVIAN.
DAVID's VOICE: (*Over the image of* VIVIAN) Not a trace of nerves. I must look whiter than any corpse.

VIVIAN, *pen in hand. She hesitates about signing. The guests joke, imitate music that's full of suspense. The bridegroom tries to deal with the situation good-humouredly.* DAVID's *voice-over still seems to speak on his behalf.*

DAVID's VOICE: Sign and get it over with!

On the point of signing, VIVIAN *looks out of frame. She sees:*

DAVID *among the guests. His expression is aggrieved and reproachful. They stare at each other. She returns to the ceremony, signs with a flourish. The guests cheer, ask the couple to kiss.* DAVID *leaves.* VIVIAN *registers his departure, but quickly joins the throng celebrating around her.*

4. STREETS, THE MALECÓN. EXT. DAY

DAVID *walking along a street. Then down another. Along the Malecón. In one hand he carries a folded newspaper which he beats against his thigh or the palm of his other hand. He looks depressed, tormented.*

DAVID's VOICE: Why did I go? Do I enjoy suffering? I had to be there, to prove it wasn't a dream. Vivian got married. Learn your lesson, David Alvarez. You'll never be happy, got it?

5. BAR. INT. DAY

A barman puts a glass of liquor down in front of DAVID. *He's absorbed in himself and doesn't look at the glass. We see the place from his perspective: a typical seedy, down-at-heel street-corner bar. Someone playing the guitar and singing.*

FIRST MAN: (*To a friend*) No woman will ever do that to me. Never, I'd kill her.

A DRUNK AT THE BAR: People who don't drink spend their whole time criticising those who do. Why do they bother, do we ever criticise them? Not never!

DAVID *eyes the liquor as if it were a laxative. He picks up the glass, tries it, intends downing the lot. The contents prove too much for him, he puts the glass on the bar, pays and walks out.*

FIRST MAN: I'd take her children away from her, kick her out of the house.

The DRUNK *pulls* DAVID's *glass in his direction.*

6. BOOKSHOP. EXT. DAY

DAVID *walks into the bookshop doorway, stops and looks at books in the shop windows. A selection of world and Latin American literature in cheap, Cuban paperback editions. He is about to go in. Decides not to, still in the doorway.*

7. CALLE 23 ON THE CORNER OF L. EXT. DAY

The pavement by the ice-cream palace, Coppelia. DIEGO *and* GERMÁN, *two homosexuals, walking along in animated conversation. Suddenly* GERMÁN *stops and points at something out of frame.* DIEGO *looks and is very pleasantly surprised. We can see:*

DAVID *walking into the gardens of the Coppelia.*

GERMÁN *elbows* DIEGO *knowingly in the ribs. The latter is delighted.*

8. THE COPPELIA ICE-CREAM PALACE

A big dish of chocolate ice-cream, intact. DAVID *sitting opposite the ice-cream, sad and withdrawn. Reminiscing.*

9. STREETS. EXT. DAY

(DAVID's *memories*)

It's been raining. DAVID *and* VIVIAN *a year earlier. They've just left the cinema and are walking along the pavement. They pass by a hoarding advertising a season of Marilyn Monroe films with pictures of her, Jack Lemmon and Joe*

Bocaza in the final scene from Some Like It Hot.
They walk down another street that is less well-lit and
crowded. She holds on to his arm and is very talkative,
carefree. We can't hear what she's saying. He's tense and
not listening. Suddenly he stops and points.
DAVID: We've arrived.

> VIVIAN *doesn't understand for a moment. She looks to*
> *where* DAVID *pointed and then understands. She looks*
> *at him somewhat surprised.*
> *They're opposite a cheap hotel, identified by a*
> *signboard and average, ill-concealed queue as a home*
> *for short-lived couples.*

10. CHEAP HOTEL: PASSAGE. INT. NIGHT
(DAVID *still reminiscing*)
DAVID *and* VIVIAN *walk along a passage inside the hotel.*
As often happens in dreams, the detail is sparse. He's
carrying the key. They are rather nervous and solemn.
They stop outside what is to be their room. DAVID *is so*
nervous he finds it difficult to open the door. He finally
succeeds with help from his shoulder.

11. CHEAP HOTEL: ROOM. INT. NIGHT
(DAVID *still reminiscing*)
VIVIAN *takes a few steps towards the centre of the room*
and stops. DAVID *stays by the door. He watches her switch*
her bag to her other hand, take a few more steps, place the
bag on the bed.
VIVIAN *inspects the place: impersonal, aseptic, cold, more*
like a surgery than a room for lovers. A bright lightbulb
inside a metal holder hangs from the ceiling, sheds a harsh
light on everything. VIVIAN *turns towards* DAVID.
VIVIAN: Was this the only place you could find?

> DAVID *looks away.*

DAVID: The place doesn't matter.

VIVIAN: Yes, it does. This makes it look as if we're doing something wrong. (*Pauses*) I never imagined anywhere like this.

She sits on the edge of the bed, her back to DAVID.

VIVIAN: Mum was right. I can't be trusted. She thinks I'm safe and sound at school and here I am in a rented back-street room with my boyfriend.

DAVID: We'd talked . . .

VIVIAN: Talking is one thing, it's quite another bringing me to a room with holes in the walls . . .

DAVID: Darling, there aren't any holes.

DAVID *notices a poorly patched hole in a rickety door. He sits next to her, and she keeps her back turned on him. He doesn't dare touch her or talk to her. He's wanting to say something, to caress her, but never gets beyond good intentions. More memories.*

12. PRE-UNIVERSITY RESIDENCE: DORMITORY FOR
SCHOLARSHIP BOYS. INT. DAY
(DAVID *still reminiscing*)

MIGUEL, DAVID's *friend and an older student, telling him how to behave in his rented room.*

MIGUEL: At the start they don't want to. But don't weaken, go down on bended knees, tell her you love her or any of that nonsense. Just wait, and if she doesn't give in, slap her a couple of times so she knows she can't fool around with you. That's what they really want. Behave like a gorilla.

13. CHEAP HOTEL: ROOM. INT. NIGHT
(DAVID *still remembering*)

DAVID *next to* VIVIAN, *looking at her. Still with her back to him. He makes an effort of will and delicately brushes her hair from her shoulder. She doesn't respond. Very delicately, he strokes her bare arm, her shoulder, waits. No*

79

*reaction. He smells her, kisses her hair, waits. No
response. He kisses her on the neck. She leans her head
slightly forward, and, aroused, he kisses her, runs his lips
along the nape of her neck. He takes her by the shoulders
and makes her turn round. She keeps her eyes lowered. He
kisses her on the lips, a long, gentle kiss which she doesn't
reciprocate. When he moves away, her eyes are still
lowered, but she's relaxed. He looks at her tenderly, takes
her hands in his. At last she looks at him lovingly,
acceptingly. This makes him happy: nervous, euphoric,
sure of himself. He smiles, sits up.*

DAVID: It's really hot, isn't it? I'm going to take my shirt
off. (*Takes it off*) Why don't you take your blouse off?

VIVIAN: Put the light out.

> DAVID *tries to put it out, but the switch doesn't work.
> That makes* VIVIAN *laugh.* DAVID *is pleased something
> has made* VIVIAN *laugh. He sits next to her and
> clumsily if gently takes her blouse off. Serious, her
> head bowed, she lets him. She's in her bra. He looks at
> her, ecstatic. Kisses her on the lips, with restrained
> passion. She responds and then their kiss becomes
> ardent.* DAVID *caresses her breasts, tries to unhook her
> bra. The clasp is awkward. She turns her back to him
> but still he can't manage. She takes it off.*
>
> VIVIAN *is naked.* DAVID *is entranced. He moves slightly
> away so he can look at her. He finds her extremely
> beautiful. Kneels on the floor in front of her breasts.
> Places his hands on hers, slides them up her arms, rests
> them on her shoulders, caresses them, stares at her
> breasts, where he suddenly sinks his face.* VIVIAN
> *embraces him, and now he can't see her, her face
> relaxes, reflects the pleasure she is feeling. She pulls*
> DAVID *against her . . .*

DAVID: VIVIAN, you're the only woman I ever want, and I

want to be the only man in your life. If only we can be allowed that much.

She invites him to kiss her breasts. He kisses one, then the other. The pleasure overwhelms VIVIAN *and she falls backwards on the bed.* DAVID *is still kneeling on the floor in front of her half-naked, half-apart legs. He's aroused by the vision. He eases his erect cock taking care she doesn't see it. Places his hands on* VIVIAN'S *knees.*

DAVID'S VOICE: Please God, help me not to behave like a gorilla.

He slips his hands upwards. Stops at the edge of her skirt. Is about to go underneath. Holds back. Is about to push her skirt up. Holds back. Moves over the material, towards her sex, but not touching it although it's within reach. Kisses her thighs through the material.

VIVIAN *is enjoying herself. She sits up, he goes in search of her mouth, but forcefully she takes his head and directs it towards her sex, and presses them together. Then, she yanks his head by the hair towards her, kisses him on the mouth, her tongue in hot pursuit of his. Without separating out, they find a better position for kissing. He tries to regain the initiative, She lowers her hand, goes after his cock. She finds it and squeezes it.* DAVID *moves her away, half frightened half-happy, embarrassed by his erection. She looks down. He's very happy, kisses her affectionately, caresses her and pushes her hair to one side.*

DAVID: You won't feel any pain or get pregnant. I swear you won't. Don't be afraid. And if you do, don't worry. We'll get married, or do whatever you want. (*He forces her to look him in the eyes, puts his heart and soul into it*) Perhaps I shouldn't say this: I love you, Vivian, I love you so much. *She pulls him towards her and they kiss on the mouth. They move apart.*

82

DAVID: All I want is to be able to love you and for you to love me.

VIVIAN: I must go to the bathroom.

DAVID lets her get up. She smiles down at him affectionately, mischievously. DAVID is happy and watches her go into the bathroom. Once inside she has to push against the door to shut it properly. DAVID is cheerful and aroused. He turns his back to the camera and eases his cock. Peers out of the window. Looks into the street. He can see:

– The city. The street. A neon sign for the Committees for the Defence of the Revolution: a vigilant eye firing arrows out in every direction which keep flashing on and off.

– A red sign on a distant building: 'Revolution is Construction'

He goes back to the centre of the room: arranges the cushions, hopelessly tries to make the things on the bedside-table look something special: a roll of toilet-paper, a tray with two glasses and a battered tin jug. He looks at the hole in the rickety door. Takes a piece of toilet roll, grabs a fragile-looking chair and after testing it out climbs up to reach the hole. He's about to close it off, but first takes a look and sees:

– a woman with huge tits astride her male, gesticulating and pulling at her hair as if she's gone crazy. Her man is making her cry out in ecstasy.

WOMAN: Ohh! Fantastic! Ohh!

DAVID moves away in disgust. It's just the kind of sex he doesn't want to have with VIVIAN. Covers over the hole as much as he can. Takes the chair back to where it was. The light projected into the room as the bathroom door opens makes him turn round. In the stream of light we see:

83

VIVIAN *appears like a goddess.* DAVID *is overwhelmed. She holds her clothes against her chest. Without looking at* DAVID, *she goes to the bed, drops her clothes on the floor and gets under the sheet. When he starts walking towards her, she turns to the wall, her back bare down to the start of her buttocks. He stops in the middle of the room in rapt contemplation. Her half-nakedness sends waves of tenderness and desire through him.*

14. COPPELIA. EXT. DAY
The chocolate ice-cream has started to melt. DAVID *comes down to earth. His memories make him suffer, feel ashamed, as if they related to something very unpleasant.*

15. CHEAP HOTEL: ROOM. INT. NIGHT
(DAVID *still reminiscing*)
DAVID *and* VIVIAN *in the same position as in the previous scene. Rather inhibited,* DAVID *strips off, sits on the edge of the bed. He looks inhibited, but happy and determined. Just as he's about to pull off the sheet or take her by the shoulder to turn her over, she speaks to him harshly, destroying the magic of the situation.*
VIVIAN: So this is why you asked me to go to the cinema with you.
DAVID *is crushed by this outburst.*

16. COPPELIA. EXT. DAY
DAVID *in* COPPELIA, *fidgets. He can hardly stand the pain brought on by his memories.*
DAVID's VOICE: Why didn't God tell her I was the last person she could accuse of anything like that?

17. CHEAP HOTEL: ROOM. INT. NIGHT
(DAVID *still reminiscing*)

The scene just after VIVIAN *has spoken out. She turns round and speaks harshly to him.*

VIVIAN: It was a lie from start to finish. The invitation to the cinema, your 'Let's go for a little walk', everything.
   DAVID *is extremely hurt by what she says, by her tone of voice.*

DAVID: I love you, Vivian.

VIVIAN: And you show your love by bringing me to this kind of place. You're only interested in sex, like all the rest of them.

DAVID: You're what matters to me.

VIVIAN: Well, you show me then.
   Recovering his self-respect, DAVID *gets up, grabs his trousers and energetically starts pulling them on.* VIVIAN *is slightly dismayed, perhaps she has taken things too far.*

DAVID: Show you? I won't touch you till the day we get married. In a room in a five-star hotel. (*He's pulled his trousers on, and looks at her*) Aren't you going to get dressed?
   We hear DIEGO's *voice.*

DIEGO's VOICE: Scuse me, sweetie.

18. COPPELIA. EXT. DAY

DAVID *comes down to earth. Looks at the person who has just spoken to him and is taken aback.* DIEGO *is opposite him, with a dish of strawberry ice-cream. His homosexual get-up is obvious and shocks* DAVID.

DAVID: (*To himself*) I don't believe it!
   DIEGO *smiles at* DAVID, *places his ice-cream on the table and starts arranging his numerous packages, that in the end take up two empty chairs and part of the table. They include a camera and a bunch of sunflowers.* DAVID *looks around. He sees an empty table nearby. We can see* GERMÁN *in the background,*

looking intently on. (During the sequence there are one or two intercut images of GERMÁN.)

DIEGO *finally settles in.* DAVID *notices his dish of chocolate ice-cream is intact.* DIEGO *looks at him, very friendly and dreamy-eyed, and then talks about his ice-cream but in a very ambiguous tone of voice.*

DIEGO: I couldn't resist the temptation . . . I adore strawberries.

DAVID once again stares at the empty table. He would obviously prefer to change tables, but some children come and sit there. He looks at DIEGO *as contemptuously as possible, puts his newspaper in the middle of the table to mark out the two halves, and starts to eat his ice-cream at top speed.*

DIEGO: Watch out, baby! You'll choke on it.

DAVID automatically slows down his ice-cream eating. He gets an attack of coughing.

DIEGO: I told you so. Have some of this. (*He offers him his glass of water*)

DAVID drinks from his own. He returns to his ice-cream rather more calmly.

DIEGO: All over with, darling?

He takes out some brightly-coloured paper serviettes, drapes one over DAVID. *He knocks it on the floor.* DIEGO *pretends not to notice his reaction and drapes another one on him.*

DIEGO: Temper! Temper!

DAVID ignores the serviette. DIEGO *gives him another long, simpering look, scoops up a blob of ice-cream on to the tip of his spoon and puts it in his mouth. He makes a meal out of it.*

DIEGO: Dee-li-cious. (*To* DAVID) It's the only decent thing they make in this country. (*Softly*) Soon it'll be for export only and we'll be on sugared water.

DAVID *concentrates tensely on his ice-cream.* DIEGO
yelps in delight. He has found an almost whole
strawberry. DAVID *glances in his direction.*

DIEGO: Ooh! (*He picks the strawberry up between the tips*
of his fingers. Looks at DAVID *meaningfully.* Today is
my lucky day: I keep finding tasty morsels.

DAVID, *getting nearer to break-point, controls himself.*
DIEGO *puts the strawberry on the edge of his plate.*

DIEGO: (*To the strawberry*) We'll keep you till last. And if
someone wants a taste, we won't be selfish.(*To*
DAVID)Anybody want any? (*As he gets no response*)
He's dumb. (*Looks in his bags*) OK, let's fly on the
wings of the imagination, as we can't fly any other
way. We're on the boulevard of Montmartre, next to
Notre Dame, behind the Champs Elysées. Où est *Le*
Cahier du Cinema? (*He takes a magazine out*) Voilà!
He pushes his ice-cream to one side and moves a pile
of books from his lap to the table as near as possible
to DAVID. *He sits back in his chair and pretends to*
lose himself in his magazine.

DIEGO: Summer fashions!

DAVID, *irritated, eyes* DIEGO: *pose, appearance,*
wardrobe. Then he looks at the books. With interest.
They are good-quality foreign editions. He looks at
DIEGO, *who seems absorbed in his magazine, and*
strains to read the titles of the books. DIEGO *turns a*
page and returns to his ice-cream. Then DAVID *goes*
back to the books. Shot of a front-cover upside down
in relation to DAVID: Conversación en la catedral,
Mario Vargas Llosa. DAVID *is enthused by the title.*
When he looks up, DIEGO *is eying him keenly.*

DIEGO: I'd better put them away, hadn't I? Scuse me.

DAVID *acts as if he's not interested and returns to his*
ice-cream. DIEGO *puts the books away in a bag.*

DIEGO: That was unforgiveably rash of me. You know what'll happen? Our police are really cultured. If one comes by and catches us with this lot we'll be cutting cane tomorrow.

DAVID *looks daggers at him.*

DIEGO: No joking. The things this gentleman says about Communism! If you want I'll lend it to you . . . At home I've got the complete works of Severo Sarduy and Goytisolo.

DAVID *scowls at him.*

DIEGO: Is Vargas Llosa the one you're interested in? This one's dedicated to me, but I've got another copy. Shall we go and get it? I only live round the corner.

DAVID: I don't visit the houses of strangers.

DIEGO: Don't miss out, darling, don't be foolish. Where else will you get these books?

DAVID *moves his red membership card of the Young Communists from one shirt pocket to the other.* DIEGO *registers the action and looks around as if to make sure nobody is listening.*

DIEGO: (*Confidentially*) I get it. You can only read books authorised by the Young Communists. Put a cover on them, honey, use your imagination!

DAVID: I don't have to put a cover on anything, I can read whatever I want. And I don't feel like talking. Get it?

DIEGO: We are moody! Were you on guard duty last night? Those guard duties!

MIGUEL *joins the queue to buy tickets for ice-creams.* DIEGO *at the table renews his attack.*

DIEGO: I know who you are.

DAVID *looks at him.*

DIEGO: That's right. I've seen you lots of times leaving the University.

DAVID: Not me.

DIEGO: Come on, dear, course it was you.

DAVID: (*Upset*) It wasn't!

DIEGO: Oh, do forgive me . . . Comrade *Thorvald* . . .
The word Thorvald throws DAVID *into total disarray.*
He looks at DIEGO in consternation.

DIEGO: (*Humbly*) I only wanted to show you a few books
. . . and some photos from the time you acted in *A
Doll's House* in that Festival.

DAVID: You've got photos of the play?

DIEGO: Lots of them. You look wonderful. Everyone I
show them to goes crazy about you, really crazy.

DAVID: You can't have any photos of me, and even less be
showing them around. Where did you get them?

DIEGO: I'm a photographer.

DAVID: You've got to give them to me.

DIEGO: Of course. Let's go and get them.

DAVID: Where do you live?

DIEGO: Just round the corner, with my parents and some
maiden aunts who never go out.
DAVID *can see* MIGUEL *buying his tickets. Because of
the lay-out of the ice-cream palace, he will inevitably
come and sit down in the area where they are.*

DAVID: Let's go and get them. You must give them all to
me with the negatives. (*He gets up*) Come on. (*Sees
that the only exit will force him to meet* MIGUEL)

DIEGO: Let me finish my ice-cream.

DAVID: Get on with it then. Don't talk to me in the street.
(*He jumps over the fence and walks off.*)
DIEGO *hurriedly gathers his things up and runs after*
DAVID. GERMÁN, *amazed by his speedy conquest, goes
over to the table. He picks up the strawberry left on
the edge of the plate and eats it.*

19. DIEGO's HOUSE: STREET. EXT. DAY
A taxi, an American car from the 50s, judders and snorts

to a halt in front of the building where DIEGO lives in Old Havana.

20. TAXI. INT. DAY
DAVID *and* DIEGO *in the front seat, the latter next to the window. Four passengers in the back.* DAVID *has to hold on to the flowers which* DIEGO *hands to him while he looks for money to pay the taxi. The* DRIVER *maliciously registers the relationship between them.*
DRIVER: (*Taking the money*) For the pair of you?
DIEGO: Keep the change.(*He gets out*)
    DAVID *stays put, looks as if he's not going to get off.*
DIEGO: Come on, sweetie. You've got to get your book.
    DAVID *can't make his mind up. The driver and passengers are waiting for him.*
WOMAN PASSENGER: Get a move on, sweetie, make your mind up, I'm getting frazzled in this tin can.
    DAVID *has no choice but to get off. The passengers keep up their banter.*
WOMAN PASSENGER: Both of them ought to be cutting cane.
MALE PASSENGER: My nephew's off doing his Military Service and this lot as free as the wind.

21. DIEGO'S HOUSE: STREET. EXT. DAY
DAVID *on the pavement, holding the bunch of flowers. He hands them to* DIEGO, *who points the way in. A group of* PIONEERS *walks along the pavement behind their schoolmistress right into their path. They have to wait. The* PIONEERS *are singing.*

22. DIEGO'S HOUSE: ENTRANCE-HALL. INT. DAY
DAVID *and* DIEGO *reach the lift out of which steps a* MAN *carrying a rabbit.* DIEGO *walks in,* DAVID *stays outside. It is an old manually controlled lift cage.*

92

DAVID: I'll go up, but I warn you: don't get any wrong ideas about me.

DIEGO: Ooh, now what wrong ideas might they be, dearie? As if.

DAVID goes in. When DIEGO goes to shut the door, he can see NANCY, holding a bunch of red flowers, walking into the entrance. When she sees the lift, she runs towards it. DIEGO shuts the door and presses the button.

NANCY: The lift! The lift!

DAVID: Wait for her.

DIEGO: She's on our Vigilance Committee.

DAVID: So what?

NANCY'S VOICE: Make sure you close it.

DIEGO: I don't like her.

23. THE DEN: PASSAGEWAY, SITTING-ROOM. INT.DAY

DIEGO and DAVID walk down the passageway. It's an old hotel that's been turned into homes. Most of the doors are open and there's a lot of coming and going of neighbours and children, everybody about their daily business. Above the typically Cuban noise, a mainly salsa-style music blares out. DIEGO reaches his door and unlocks it.

DIEGO: Come in. Welcome to The Den, a place where not everybody finds a welcome.

DAVID walks in, DIEGO switches on the light, and DAVID suddenly finds himself confronted by the decor of The Den. To DAVID's mind it is a strange, untidy, extravagant place, but fascinating all the same. The walls are covered with shelves laden with books, pictures, posters, photos, masks and the most attractive, random objects. Mobiles, objects, and rattles hang down from the ceiling. Though everything is in apparent disorder, each object has its rightful place and significance, and in spite of its motley appearance, the room is pleasant and spacious enough

94

for one person. A rustic staircase leads up to the bedroom (a Havanan loft).

The Cuban Altar is in the background (we have the whole film to describe this). It is not devoted to gods but to Art, nationality, Cubanity. It comprises the most diverse motifs within Cuban culture focusing on the deepest syncretism of the African and the Spanish, the cultured and the popular. One can admire anything from ballet shoes to 'lucky' charms, photos of nineteenth-century poets, images of San Lázaro and San Juan Bosco, and even faces and images of beautiful Creoles simply cut out of newspapers and magazines. Stuck or pinned to the walls are pages of books, newspaper headlines, poems or sentences handwritten on plain sheets of paper, from Epicurus to the barman from the street-corner. It is an exuberant, 'personal' altar conceived in the style of the painter Leandro Soto, with a dash of Raúl Martínez. There is only one bare wall, occupied by a large image of the Virgin of Charity and patron saint of Cuba, in front of whom there are offerings and a lighted candle. That's where the staircase is. On another wall, or perhaps on the door to the street, there is a poster of Some Like It Hot similar to the one on the hoarding we have already seen, which, because of its position, will often show up behind characters in the course of the film.

The place exercises a strong, contradictory influence on DAVID. What first impresses and scares him are some fairly large sculptures, with vigorous expressions, most of them covered in sheets. They are pieces for GERMÁN's exhibition that DIEGO is storing for a few days. Then there are the books, which catch DAVID's attention.

DIEGO: (While he puts his packets away, moves the most

inconveniently placed sculptures, opens the door on to the balcony, puts his flowers in a jug, etc.)
Forgive the mess. These sculptures are wonderful. Germán, who created them, is a genius, though it may not look that way. We are preparing an exhibition that's going to create a stir. We are short of a few things but a friend from an embassy is going to help. Sit in that armchair.

DAVID: Where are the people who live here?

DIEGO: (*Shouting out to some inner room*) Mum, dad, grandma, Auntie Chucha, Twins . . .(*Nobody replies*) They've gone to join a queue. (*He goes to shut the door*)

DAVID: Don't!

DIEGO: Just as you like. That way we make life easier for the neighbours.
As soon as he is in the flat, DIEGO's *mannered behaviour loses the aggression of the Coppelia. He becomes relaxed and easy-going.*

DIEGO: I'll make the tea: to lower the tension.

DAVID: I don't drink tea. Give me the photos.

DIEGO: I'll have to look them out.(*He points to the endless piles of paper. Pretends he is trying to remember where, in the face of so much paper. Picks out two enormous bundles and places them on the table*) I think they're here, you check. I'll make the tea, I mustn't neglect such an important guest.
He heads for the kitchen. As he passes by the Virgin he gives her a knowing smile and says in a low voice:

DIEGO: Thanks, my love. You've earned yourself a box of candles.
DAVID *is left alone. Looks at the packets.*

DIEGO'S VOICE: (*Apparently fighting with a dog*) Rocco, what about that mess? You're really stupid! I'm getting fed up with you! That's the last time I'll tell you.
DAVID *goes over to the table. He picks up an envelope*

*and takes out the contents. They are male nude
photos. He puts them back immediately. When he
hears* DIEGO's *voice he moves away from the table.*

DIEGO'S VOICE: If they're not there, they'll be in those
boxes. We'll look them out in a minute.

In one corner of the room, DAVID *can see various old
boxes stuffed to bursting with books and papers. He
goes over to the armchair mentioned by* DIEGO, *which
preserves some of its antique character despite being
old and battered. Really fascinated, he sits down and
starts examining the walls. In particular he looks at
shelves packed with books, that all look as if they've
been read, as if their owner loves them.*

DIEGO: (*Out of frame*) When I'm going to read John
Donne and Cavafy I sit in that armchair.

(*He walks in*) Only at moments such as those. How
can a country progress if its youth hasn't heard of
John Donne or Cavafy?

(*He takes two well-thumbed books from a shelf, shows
them to him*) Look at the state they're in. I'm the only
person in Havana who owns translations of their work
and I never tire of circulating them among young
people. I'll put you on my waiting-list.

(*He returns the books to their shelf and goes back into
the kitchen*)

DAVID *resumes his investigations. His attention is drawn
by some objects that evidently come from abroad,
including a magazine rack with copies of* Ramparts,
Paris Match, Time, Playboy, *etc. He takes a copy of a
magazine. Puts it down as soon as* DIEGO *says something.*

DIEGO'S VOICE: Do you take lemon in your tea?

DAVID: I told you I don't drink tea. I haven't got stomach-
ache. Leave that and look for the photos, I've got to
be somewhere at five o'clock.

DIEGO: (*From the kitchen*) Well I can offer you coffee.
(*He comes in*) Tea is a drink for civilised people. But
we prefer coffee.
(*He sings*) 'Ay, mamá Inés; ay, mamá Inés; all us
blacks drink coffee.'
(*Goes over to the record-player*) I'll put some music
on. That way the neighbours can't listen in on our
conversation. The Vigilance Committee woman told
me to do that. And someone from Security told her.

DAVID: Let the neighbours listen.

DIEGO: Who do you prefer? María Callas, Teresa Stratas,
Renata Tebaldi? Or Celina González?

DAVID *responds with silence.* DIEGO *puts on a María
Callas record. He listens in ecstasy for a few seconds.*

DIEGO: My God, why can't this Island come up with a
voice like that. We're badly in need of another voice. If
not, we're stuck with María Remolá for the duration.
(*Strikes an operatic pose*) 'Neighbour, the ooooonion's
cooooome.' (*Exits theatrically to the kitchen*)

DAVID *returns to the pile of photos and quickly looks
through two or three sets.*

NANCY *appears at the door.*

NANCY: Have the onions come?
(*She's surprised when she sees* DAVID. *His looks make
an impact. She looks at him admiringly*) Excuse me, I
thought young Diego was by himself.
(*Still taken aback*) As I saw the door was open . . .
(*She smiles at him, takes one last glance, and leaves*)

24. DIEGO'S HOUSE: PASSAGEWAY. INT. DAY
NANCY, *once in the passageway, reveals the favourable
impact* DAVID *has made.*

NANCY: A sight for sore eyes!

25. THE DEN: SITTING-ROOM. INT. DAY

DIEGO *in the doorway to the kitchen*

DIEGO: Who was that?

DAVID: The Vigilance Committee woman.

DIEGO: (*Goes to the door and closes it*) What did I tell you?

DAVID: Give me the photos then.

DIEGO: (*Runs to the kitchen*) The coffee's boiling over!

> DAVID *stands in the middle of the room, annoyed with himself.* DIEGO *brings in a tray set out with tea-pot, cups, sugar bowl and one flower in a small jug.*

DIEGO: Sit down.

> DAVID *sits down.* DIEGO *holds the tray in one hand and grips a small table in the other as he walks over to* DAVID. *Suddenly, he stumbles and spills the cup of coffee over* DAVID, *staining his shirt in a big way. (As we later discover, it was a fake stumble, juggling on* DIEGO's *part.)* DAVID *jumps to his feet.*

DIEGO: Christ! Did I scald you?

> DAVID *looks at his stained shirt.*

DIEGO: What a mess. I'm really sorry. Take it off and I'll wash it rightaway! It comes out if you catch it quick.

> DAVID *takes it off uneasily.*

DIEGO: Come on, hand it over. Such a shame.

> As he takes the shirt, he stares at DAVID's *naked torso.*

DAVID: Get me something to put on.

> DIEGO *opens a drawer and throws him a yellow towel. He runs off to the bathroom.*

DAVID: My best shirt!

> Upset, he paces around. Sits down again in John Donne's armchair, wrapping the towel round himself. DIEGO *takes* DAVID's *shirt straight from the bathroom to the balcony.*

DAVID: That was quick!

DIEGO: Right, I've got a special stain-remover. Don't
worry. It won't leave even a shadow.
In DAVID'*s line of vision, we can see* DIEGO *hanging
the shirt out.* DAVID *looks away when he sees him
coming back. He's more on edge than ever.*

DIEGO: (*In the sitting-room*) I really am sorry. Please
forgive me. I'm very clumsy. I don't know how it
happened. (*He looks at the tray. Cheers up*) Luckily it
was only the coffee that was spilt. I know: I've got a
real good pick-me-up for you.
*He goes over to a small cabinet, opens it and takes out
two very beautiful tea-cups. He pours the tea out and
offers one to* DAVID.

DIEGO: Try this tea. It's Indian.
DAVID *takes the cup. He still doesn't try a sip.* DIEGO
*walks over towards him. There are also cakes and
chocolate biscuits. Finally he pulls up a chair and sits
down.*

DIEGO: Dostoevsky's characters drank tea. As for the
English . . . now, at five pm the whole of Great Britain
gathers round the tea-table. What time is it?

DAVID: (*Looks at his watch*) Five o'clock.

DIEGO: Pure magic! (*Picks up his cup of tea*) Try some and
tell me what you think.
DAVID *takes a sip.* DIEGO *looks on expectantly.*

DIEGO: Well?

DAVID: It's not sweet enough.

DIEGO: No! That would be criminal. Take another sip.
DAVID *does so but is not overly impressed.*

DIEGO: Just imagine. The cup is Sèvres china. How about
that? You are drinking tea from a Sèvres tea-cup that
belonged to the Loynaz del Castillo family. Isn't that
terrific? Out there people pushing and shoving on the
buses, blacks shouting their heads off and you and me

101

in here, listening to María Callas and drinking Indian tea from Sèvres china.

DAVID: You're a racist.

DIEGO: Me a racist? In no way. I know what a black's worth. (*Pause*) Not a tea party. One blink, and whoosh, your black's disappeared and your Sèvres china with him.

DAVID *can't help showing he finds the remark amusing.*

DAVID: Thanks to the Revolution, there's no racism in this country. We come from Africa, in case you didn't know.

DIEGO: They do. You and I don't, we're from Spain . . . Those gypsy eyes didn't come from Nigeria or Senegal, my darling. Your grandad brought them from Andalusia.

DAVID: Look, I can't spend the afternoon listening to this rubbish. Is my shirt dry?

DIEGO: Quite right. Let's be serious. What's your handle?

DAVID *doesn't understand that remark.*

DIEGO: We haven't introduced ourselves. I'm Diego. People always crack the joke, 'Dig you, Diego.' It's like Dick, they always say 'Dirty Dick'. What's your name?

DAVID: Juan Carlos Rondón, at you service.

DIEGO: You're a liar. You're David.

DAVID *is taken aback.*

DIEGO: I know everything about everybody. That's to say, about the people worth knowing. Come on, what do you want to talk about? I don't want to force a subject on you.

DAVID *doesn't respond and looks the other way.*

DIEGO: Can't you think of anything? Have you read Oscar Wilde? Gide? Lorca? Don't tell me you wouldn't have been delighted to spend an afternoon chatting to them?

DAVID: Well . . . I'm not sure.

DIEGO: Of course you would! Look, they all had
'something' in common with me . . .
DAVID *is astonished.*
DIEGO: Didn't you know? And they're not the only ones.
The most renowned, the bravest warriors as well.
Alexander the Great loved Hefaestion; and Achilles
had Patroclus . . . he was his mainstay. (DIEGO *gets up
and goes to a bookshelf*) It's a long list, dearie. They
even say that Hemingway . . . You know, the guy who
liked rifles and lion-hunting.
DAVID *doesn't believe him.* DIEGO *takes a heavy tome
off the shelf.*
DIEGO: A Marxist treatise on sexuality. (*Opens it and
pretends to read*) It argues that 60 per cent of men have
a homosexual experience at some time in their life,
without damaging their personalities. A. Raskolnikov. If
even they say so . . . (*Returns the book to the shelf*)
DAVID: I belong to the other 40 per cent.
DIEGO: (*He sits down opposite* DAVID) The best option is to
try every flavour and take it as it comes. (*He crosses his
legs, relaxes*) I'll tell you how I became a queer.
DAVID *gets up violently.* DIEGO *takes fright.*
DAVID: That's enough! I don't have to listen to this! (*He
goes on the balcony and grabs his wet shirt*) I told you
not to get the wrong idea about me!
DIEGO: Hold it, sweetie, don't get into a sweat. You've
misunderstood me. Come on, what were you thinking?
DAVID *averts his gaze and rushes across the room
towards the door.*
You can't go yet. We've not found your photos. Or
Vargas Llosa's book. David!
DAVID *slams the door behind him.* DIEGO *looks
confused. Suddenly he gets furious with himself.
Squares up to the Virgin.*

DIEGO: Fuck! You let me open up and squawk like a parrot. And in Coppelia I performed like a dockside queen. (*He removes a plate of offerings*) Bring him back, bring him back or I'll put you on bread and water. (*To the three Juans in a boat*) And as for you, I hope the coastguards catch you.

26. STREET, BUS STOP. EXT. DAY
DAVID *walks in between the other pedestrians, disgusted with himself.*
DAVID'S VOICE: I did the right thing. I didn't take his book and I told him to get lost. He was lying about the photos. The son of a bitch. They should send them all to work in the fields.
Suddenly he slows down. Stops. Notices his reflection in a shop window getting clearer and clearer. His reflected image looks at him seriously, reproachfully.
DAVID *gets embarrassed, looks away and starts to walk slowly, hesitantly. What he listens to now rather than his voice is his Conscience.*
DAVID'S VOICE: How easily you solve your spot of bother, David Alvarez. (*ironically*) You didn't take the book and you told him to get lost. When did you tell him to get lost? You went into the house of a queer! And you're an active Communist! Is that the thanks the Revolution gets for all it's done for you?
He reaches the stop. Walks up and down. He has no answers for the accusations from his Conscience. The bus comes and DAVID *joins the group fighting to get on.*

27. STUDENT RESIDENCE: MIGUEL'S ROOM. INT. DAY
MIGUEL, *in bed reading a book of Political Economy. He is a well-built, handsome guy, who resembles, or thinks he resembles, James Dean. There's a photo of the actor by his*

104

bedside and he imitates the way he smokes. He puts his book down and smiles at DAVID *as he comes in.*

DAVID: (*Solemnly*) I've just had a real spot of bother.

MIGUEL'S *interest is alerted by* DAVID'S *expression and tone of voice.* DAVID *sits down in a chair opposite his bed.*

DAVID: I was eating an ice-cream this afternoon in Coppelia when this guy came in and sat down at my table. A strange guy.

MIGUEL: What kind of strange guy?

DAVID: A queer.

MIGUEL: (*Smiling*) How do you know he was a queer?

DAVID *is slightly disconcerted. He waves his hand in the air.*

DAVID: There was chocolate and he ordered strawberry . . . But not only that. If he'd just been a queer I'd have left or I'd have clouted him one. You know how I can't stand them.

MIGUEL: (*Trying to make a joke*) He probably fancied you.

DAVID: (*Doesn't go along with the joke*) He started to make fun of the Revolution.

MIGUEL: (*Solemnly*) And you let him?

DAVID: I wouldn't have in other circumstances; but something made me suspect he was involved in some shady dealing.

MIGUEL: What happened then?

DAVID: I let him talk. In the end he invited me to his house.

MIGUEL: Come on, David, he was after something else.

DAVID: No, he wasn't. Do you think I was born yesterday? First he showed me some foreign literary works you can't get in the shops, and then used the books as a pretext to invite me to his place.

MIGUEL: How did he know that you liked literature?
   DAVID *looks rather embarrassed. But immediately regains his composure.*
DAVID: Apparently he cruises the university. By the time he makes a pass at someone he's already found out a thing or two about him.
MIGUEL: Did you go?
DAVID: It was up to me to find out if he was into anything shady, wasn't it?
MIGUEL: Of course.
DAVID: He's got a library stuffed with magazines and books written by counter-revolutionaries and spends his time circulating them among the youth. He wanted me to take some off with me.
   He can see how interested MIGUEL *is in what he's just said and climbs into his bunk.*
DAVID: He's getting an exhibition ready with a friend.
MIGUEL: What kind of exhibition?
DAVID: Some very peculiar, semi-religious sculptures. He's getting help from an Embassy.
MIGUEL: (*Alarmed*) From an Embassy? Fuck, David, this is serious.

28. STUDENT RESIDENCE: WASH-ROOMS. INT. DAY
DAVID *is having a shower. A powerful jet of water is falling on his face, forehead, neck, as if purifying him. His eyes are closed and he is enjoying the water. His face wears an expression of relief, of pleasure. He switches the shower off, opens his eyes, shakes his head. Suddenly, he turns serious, his face darkens once more.*
DAVID: For fuck's sake, am I or am I not turning into a lousy son of a bitch?

106

29. HAVANA: STREETS, PARK, HOUSE WHERE VIVIAN LIVES. DAY

The city, people. A less pleasant shot than in the opening sequence. Tired people; indolent people; happy people; idle people. A number of couples caressing and kissing for all to see, at times delicately, at others brazenly. Included in the previous, the odd sign or hoarding of the kind: 'Every man has the right to get tired but then has no right to be a man in the vanguard' 'Imperialist gentlemen you don't scare us.'

When we come to DAVID *it is obvious that he is looking at the city with a degree of depression. He's sitting in a park and should look repeatedly, expectantly, at a well-defined spot: the elegant façade of the two-storey house where* VIVIAN *lives.*

Over the above images, DAVID's *thoughts.*

DAVID'S VOICE: What will I be doing in ten years' time? What will have become of this city? What will the people be like? I can see how carefree everyone is. Or couldn't they care less? Do they like someone else to do their thinking and deciding for them? (*Over the image of a couple kissing*) Sex is this country's drug, it's a way to avoid thinking, to let oneself go.(*Over* VIVIAN's *house*) She got married! Just my luck. She's going to bed with him. Perhaps right now.

We see him depressed on the park bench. He looks towards the building and suddenly stands up. He can see: VIVIAN *leaving the building.*

30. COMMERCIAL AREA: ARCADES, SHOPS. EXT. DAY

DAVID *follows* VIVIAN *through the arcades in a shopping area. She goes into a shop.* DAVID *watches her through the window talking to a shop assistant. As she leaves they bump into each other in the arcade. He pretends to be surprised.*

DAVID: What a coincidence!

She gives him a beautiful smile.

VIVIAN: No coincidence. You were following me.

DAVID looks embarrassed. She takes pleasure in his embarrassment, but then gives him a friendly smile. She takes him by the arm.

VIVIAN: Let's go for a drink.

31. CAFETERIA. INT. DAY

DAVID and VIVIAN seated at a table, serious and silent. They're not looking at each other. Suddenly he speaks gently but with determination.

DAVID: Couldn't you wait?

She turns and looks him in the eye. Speaks harshly, a tone she knows to be cruel, but necessary.

VIVIAN: I couldn't. I wanted to be a woman. I tired of virginity.

DAVID is shocked for a second. He recovers.

DAVID: And now you tell me? I knew perfectly well what had to be done. That wasn't what we talked about. You asked me to leave sex for later, for when we finished our studies.

VIVIAN: Right. But I didn't want you to do what I said. (*Pauses. Softens. Tries to hold his hand, but he pulls away.*) I have needs you can't satisfy, David. We're the same age, but I'm a woman, and you're a boy.

DAVID: I'm no boy! What are these needs that I can't satisfy?

VIVIAN: (*She hesitates*) You've got nothing to offer. You've no house, no car and won't have for a long time. I'm sorry if that seems brutal.

DAVID: That's not the reason.

VIVIAN: It is. I'm not who you think I am. You idealise me, you idealise love. I've tried to explain things.

DAVID: I don't idealise one bit. I love you and you loved me.

VIVIAN: But now I want to have a family and I want it now, not when I'm an old woman. I couldn't wait for you.

DAVID: You were playing me along the whole time. You didn't care about me. Why can't you be straight with me?

She doesn't reply. Looks away, very upset. She's sorry to see him suffering in that way. She rekindles her love for him, looks at him with desire.

VIVIAN: As if not loving you were that easy. I sometimes think that leaving you was the biggest mistake I ever made. But another part of me tells me it wasn't. Believe me, David, you're taking a long time to grow up.

DAVID: You don't love that guy.

VIVIAN: Stop feeling sorry for yourself. I'm sure you'll find someone much better than me.

DAVID: I don't want anyone better than you.(*Looks at her despairingly, on the verge of tears*) You know I don't!

VIVIAN: See what a state you get into?

He looks away.

VIVIAN: You're not the only one suffering. How do you think I feel knowing that you spend your days in that park? (*A long pause. She takes her eyes off him in order to whisper the following*) They're sending my husband to Italy. We're going any day now. For a minimum of two years, perhaps three.

That was the worst news possible for DAVID. He looks at her distraught. She looks at him.

VIVIAN: I thought perhaps . . . Before we leave . . . I could be your lover.

DAVID: I don't want to be your lover! (*He stands up*) Don't

109

feel sorry for me: I won't keep watch on you or come
by your house any more.
*He gets up and walks off. Sadly she watches him
walk away.*

32. THE MALECÓN. EXT. DUSK
DAVID *sitting on the reefs, looks out to sea. The Malecón's
behind him. The sea is dark and turbulent.*

33. SCHOOL OF POLITICAL SCIENCES: COURTYARD. INT. DAY
In the break, DAVID *walks with fellow students but doesn't
mix in. He stands apart, leans against a wall, remains
isolated. Drinks a bottle of soft drink.*
MIGUEL'S VOICE: David!

> DAVID *looks up.* MIGUEL *is calling to him from a
> second-floor window. Solemnly, indicates he should go
> upstairs.*

34. SCHOOL OF POLITICAL SCIENCES: LECTURE THEATRE.
INT. DAY
An empty lecture theatre. MIGUEL, *his arm round* DAVID's
shoulder, accompanies him to the window.
MIGUEL: I investigated that business of yours.
DAVID: Which business?
MIGUEL: With the queer.
DAVID: Oh, forget it. I'd forgotten all about that. I made it
    out to be more important than it really was.
MIGUEL: Are you crazy? You gave it exactly the right
    amount of importance. You must find out more.
DAVID: Find out more about what?
MIGUEL: About everything. About the exhibition, about the
    Embassy. Think up an excuse to go back to the
    queer's place, get on close terms, become one of his
    friends.

110

DAVID: I'm not doing anything of the sort. Forget the whole business.

MIGUEL: David, this is serious: do you think you can expect anything good to come from an individual who isn't even faithful to his own sex?

His question makes an impression on DAVID.

35. DIEGO'S HOUSE: STREET. EXT. DAY

DAVID *is watching the building. He's holding a folded newspaper and drinking fresh lemonade. He sees* DIEGO *shut the door to the balcony. Gets ready to follow him.* DIEGO *leaves the building with his usual bags and umbrella.*

36. STREET, GOMEZ'S BLOCK . EXT. INT. DAY

DAVID *follows* DIEGO *who goes into* GOMEZ's *block.* DAVID *does as well. Lots of people coming and going.* DIEGO *stops to chat to a young, handsome male whom he clearly 'knows from behind'.* DAVID *takes advantage of the opportunity to walk on.* DIEGO *says goodbye to the youth and then* DAVID *walks over towards him pretending to read the newspaper.* DIEGO *walks past without seeing him.* DAVID *stops, hesitates. He calls him, just loud enough to be heard.*

DAVID: Psst, Diego.

DIEGO *turns round. Is surprised and astonished.*

37. THE DEN. INT. DAY

DIEGO *comes into frame, by the corner with the Virgin, whom he looks at gratefully.*

DIEGO: (*Softly, to the Virgin*) Mummy, you've worked a miracle. You won't be sorry.

We can see DAVID *standing in the middle of the sitting-room, looking at* GERMÁN's *sculptures, covered in sheets.*

111

DAVID: When does your friend's exhibition start?

DIEGO: I'll just put the water on for the tea. (*He goes out to the kitchen*)

DAVID: I'll sit down in that poet's armchair. What was his name?

DIEGO'S VOICE: John Dunne. Never say Donne.

DAVID: (*Sits down*) Remember I'm in the queue to read him. What country is he from?

DIEGO: England.

DAVID: Is he a friend of yours?

DAVID'S VOICE: A friend?

DAVID: Do you write to each other, or what?

DIEGO: (*Comes in*) He died in 1630.

DAVID: Oh . . .

DIEGO: Don't blush. Nobody can know everything. (*Sits down opposite* DAVID) I owe you an explanation for what happened the other day.

DAVID: There's no need. I'm the one who should apologise.

DIEGO: I was being silly. I don't know what came over me, I'm not like that, I got very on edge. I have to say you're a very disturbing young man, but . . . You know? I've got this hunch: I think we can get on well together although we're different. I believe in friendship, don't you?

DAVID: Yes, I do.

DIEGO: Do you really?

DAVID: In friendship. The other thing is quite something else.

DIEGO: (*Very pleased*) Naturally, I'm talking about friendship as well. You'll see how I can control myself like anybody else. (*He stops*) This deserves more than a cup of tea. (*He goes over to a cupboard, from which he extracts two glasses and an unopened bottle of*

Johnny Walker. Shows it off proudly) Shall we make a toast . . . with drink care of the enemy?

DAVID *eyes the bottle keenly.*

DAVID: Why not?

DIEGO: I'll get some ice! (*Exits*)

As soon as he is alone, DAVID *looks at the pile of foreign magazines, takes a copy of* Time, *puts it in his bag. His eyes alight on a photo of* LEZAMA LIMA *looking reproachfully at him.*

DIEGO'S VOICE: (*Struggling with a dog*) Rocco, as soon as you're by yourself you just please yourself! You don't know me! One of these days I'll throw you over the balcony!

He comes back all smiles and holding the ice-bucket. He opens the bottle right under DAVID's *nose.*

DIEGO: First the *orishas*. (*He pours a drop on the floor in the corner of the room. He pours out the glasses, and offers* DAVID *one*) Aren't you afraid it will make you deviate ideologically?

DAVID: When one has got firm principles . . .

DIEGO: Hear, hear. (*They make a toast*) Cheers, to our next meeting.

DIEGO *takes a sip.* DAVID, *who doesn't know how to drink, gulps the lot down. He hides the effect by looking at the altar. His eyes reconnect with* LEZAMA's *photo.*

DAVID: Is that your father?

DIEGO: Oh, you're such a cutie. He's José Lezama Lima, the greatest Cuban writer of all time, a universal Cuban. In a way he is my father, and yours as well. (*Sits down*) You can't imagine how happy I feel! (*Fills* DAVID's *glass*) You can borrow any of these books, and go to the ballet as often as you want, I've got really good contacts there. And one day, I can promise

113

you this now, but you'll have to earn the honour, I'll offer you a Lezaman lunch.

DAVID: What's that? Something to eat, I imagine.

DIEGO: Something really wonderful Daddy invented You'll soon have a taste, you wicked thing. (*He pauses*) You must think I'm mad. Nobody's ever that pleased to make friends with a total stranger. Well, I am. And the fact is you're no stranger to me. (*He gets up and puts on a record of music by Lecuona*) Listen to him play that piano!

DAVID: Where's he from?

DIEGO: You're obsessed with nationalities! Cuban, dear, Lecuona. (*He sits down opposite* DAVID.) Fine, let's put our cards on the table. I want you to know the territory you're exploring right from the word go, then you can never say I was underhand. As you know, I'm . . . But that isn't all.

DAVID *pricks up his ears.*

DIEGO: I'm also a believer.

DAVID: And I'm a dialectical materialist. So no need to go into all of that.

DIEGO: (*Smiling*) Yes, but there's more to it . . . I've had problems with the system.

DAVID: What kind of problems?

DIEGO: All kinds: public outcries, shows, the neighbours spy on me, I don't take part in voluntary labour schemes, I don't do guard duty . . . (*Pause*) Although that's not why they won't leave me in peace.

DAVID: Why is it then?

DIEGO: Because for people like you people like me don't fit into this society. You can't stand us and want us to clear off. But you're all wrong about me: I was born here, I belong here, and I'm not leaving even though you torch my backside. This country isn't the property of any one individual.

115

DAVID: No, it isn't. Everyone leads their life as they want to.

DIEGO: What a magnificent idea! The Revolution needs more militants like you. Now everything's out in the open, you make your mind up. You've still got time: you can stay or go, and no hard feelings.

DAVID: I'll stay. I'll show you we Communists aren't as barbaric as you depict us.

DIEGO: Three cheers! Long live democratic Communism!

DAVID: Just one thing . . .

DIEGO: Well.

DAVID: Nothing to do with me . . . you know what people are like. I'll come here but . . .

DIEGO: Don't tell me. If I see you in the street I mustn't say hello.

DAVID: That's right. And I'd rather you'd call me David. Not 'darling', 'dearie', 'honey' or 'wild little thing'. David.

DIEGO: This deserves another toast, Da-vid . . . (*Fills the glasses to the brim*) We are setting humanity an example (*Raises the bottle of whisky*) with drink from the enemy!

38. STUDENT RESIDENCE: BATHROOM. INT. NIGHT
A lavatory. DAVID, *drunk, sicks up with the help of*
MIGUEL *who is enjoying himself all the same. They're both in their underpants.*

MIGUEL: That'll make you feel better.

He takes him to the shower, puts his head under the jet of water, forces him to wash, helping him and propping him up.

MIGUEL: Next time add some soda. Haven't you seen any films? If it's whisky, you add water.

116

39. STUDENT RESIDENCE: DAVID'S ROOM. INT. NIGHT

DAVID *and* MIGUEL *talk in* DAVID's *room. He's partly revived and drying his head with a towel.*

MIGUEL: (*Leafs through the copy of* Time). The whisky is a great clue. He obviously gets his supplies from foreigners! And this is unadulterated poison.

DAVID: He's a believer.

MIGUEL: Spawned by the devil, and they find their own.

DAVID: He doesn't do guard duty or voluntary labour. His neighbours have reported him to the police because of noise.

MIGUEL: Yes, but this thing isn't police business. We'll sort it out. What did you find out about the exhibition?

DAVID: Nothing. I kept asking him, but he won't let on.

MIGUEL: But you've got to get it out of him, one way or another.

DAVID: Don't think it's easy. He's no fool. What is obvious is that he takes an interest in youths who are culturally inclined.

MIGUEL: Wonderful! That's the way to catch him. Show him your writing.

DAVID, *upset by the suggestion.*

DAVID: I'm not getting my writing mixed up in all this.

MIGUEL: Hey, the important thing is nailing him, not your writing.

The scene ends on DAVID.

40. VIVIAN'S HOUSE: IN THE STREET. EXT. DAY

VIVIAN *and her* HUSBAND *get out of their car loaded with parcels. She deliberately hangs back as her* HUSBAND *goes into the house. Then* VIVIAN *looks in the direction of the park where we've always seen* DAVID *on watch: there is no one sitting on the bench.* VIVIAN *goes into the building.*

117

41. DIEGO'S HOUSE: STREET SCENES. EXT. DAY

The street, passers by. Life goes on with its tensions but generally one can sense a peaceful, workaday atmosphere. A lorry stops and cheerful RECRUITS *jump out and immediately start flirting with girls walking by. The occasional hoarding with an uplifting slogan.*

DAVID *walks towards* DIEGO's *house. Suddenly, an ambulance drives noisily up and out climb two stretcher-bearers with a stretcher and rush into* DIEGO's *house. There is pandemonium in the entrance.* DAVID *runs towards the building.*

The lift door opens, and inside is half the neighbourhood including an OLD MAN *carrying hens, everybody is upset and vociferating.* NANCY, *covered in blood because she has slashed her wrists, has fainted Christ-like in* DIEGO's *arms and he's trying to give her air. The stretcher-bearers take over. She's almost naked and covered in blood (some people take advantage of the situation to have a grope), and she's taken to the ambulance, followed by neighbours still offering their opinions, explaining and questioning, now mixed up with people in the street who are also expressing opinions and questions and saying what should be done. The stretcher-bearers force their way through and lift* NANCY *into the ambulance. They turn away* DIEGO *who is trying to get in.*

STRETCHER-BEARER: Family only.

DIEGO: I'm her husband. (*He spots* DAVID *in the front row of onlookers, grabs him by the arm and hauls him into the ambulance*) And he's her brother.

42. AMBULANCE. INT. DAY

DIEGO *and* DAVID *inside the ambulance. Somehow a chicken has slipped in as well.* DIEGO *looks extremely frightened.*

DIEGO: (*To* DAVID) I'm going to need you. (*To* NANCY, *as*

he takes her hand) Nancy, my love, we're here, you'll
be all right. Oh, Virgin of Charity . . .
DAVID *sees that it is* NANCY, NANCY *from the
Vigilance Committee. The ambulance goes at full pelt.*

43. HOSPITAL. INT. DAY
DAVID *looks on from a distance:* NANCY *in a bed,
surrounded by medical personnel seeing to her needs. A*
DOCTOR *trying to calm* DIEGO *down, pulls him away
and explains something to him.* DIEGO *looks towards*
DAVID.

44. HOSPITAL. INT. DAY
*A needle in an arm. Blood in the catheter. Then, a very
remorseful* DIEGO.
DIEGO: Taking your own life! Something neither God nor
    Marx can forgive. Life is struggle! If I tried to commit
    suicide every time I have a problem!
    The camera shows DIEGO *talking not to* NANCY, *but to*
    DAVID, *who is giving blood.*
DIEGO: I'm sorry I couldn't give any, they've already bled
    me dry. Let's go home and I'll cook you a steak.

45. THE DEN: SITTING-ROOM. INT. DAY
DAVID'*s eating from a well-stocked plate on the table. In
front of him, he's also got fruit, salad and a litre of milk.*
DIEGO *moves backwards and forwards and brings him
more things: jam, water, bread.*
DIEGO: I'll take her to the psychiatrist even if I have to
    drag her by the hair.
DAVID: I can't manage all of this.
DIEGO: She's lovely, but when she gets her fits of
    depression . . .
DAVID: Has she got any relatives?

DIEGO: I don't even bother telling them. They're country people. This is the fifth time, you wouldn't believe it. (*He sits at the table*) I'm so grateful to you.

DAVID: I was doing my duty. She's a comrade, a Vigilance Committee member. I gave blood when there was the earthquake in Tashkent.

DIEGO: Let's say no more about her. You can take what you can't eat to the student residence.

46. THE DEN: KITCHEN

DIEGO *finishes washing up.* DAVID *leans against the door-frame and looks at him.*

DIEGO: Now we'll sit down and have a cup of tea.

DAVID: You know tea constipates.

DIEGO: That's why nobody shits in England. (*He takes something to the refrigerator. Talks to it in annoyed tones*) Rocco, you've peed yourself again! (*He gives it a kick and it starts to work noisily again. To* DAVID) It works when it feels like it. Now what is it you are studying?

DAVID: Political Sciences.

DIEGO: Well, you shouldn't. Literature's your thing.

DAVID: One should study something useful to society. I've been able to study thanks to the Revolution, don't forget that.

DIEGO: Come off it. Vocations have to be respected. You're working against yourself. A friend of mine when he was a young child displayed tremendous talents as a pianist. But his father would have none of it because art is for pansies. Now my friend is a sixty-year-old queer who can't play the piano.

DAVID *smiles.*

DIEGO: (*Pleased to have got a smile out of him*) A smile on such a dismal day! David, I'm sorry, but you do have a

very beautiful smile . . . If it weren't for boys like you
there'd be no reason to be queer.

DAVID *looks serious.*

DIEGO: Forgive me, I can keep my promises. What's your
sign? Let me guess. (*He looks at him*) VIRGO!

DAVID *nods.*

DIEGO: That's wonderful for a writer. The force of destiny,
my dear. I'm Scorpio and Rocco is Leo. Listen to that
roar. *The refrigerator gives a bad-tempered grunt.*

47. THE DEN: SITTING-ROOM. INT. NIGHT

Music: Adiós a Cuba *by Ignacio Cervantes.* DAVID *is sitting
in John Donne's armchair opposite the table where the tea-
service is laid out. There are small cakes and biscuits.*

DIEGO: Look how simple and pleasant life can be. Tell me,
why don't we have places in Havana where you can sit
down, drink a cup of tea and talk to friends. Is that
going to lead to the collapse of Communism?

DAVID: There are more pressing needs than drinking tea,
and they've been sorted.

DIEGO: Oh I know: the Revolution has brought equality;
and if we compare ourselves to the Third World the
statistics are conclusive. But you tell me, where can
people go to talk about their good fortune? Wherever
you go you're treated badly or they won't let you in.
(*He can see* DAVID *doesn't like the subject of
conversation*) Let's forget politics.

DAVID *concentrates on the music, which is coming to
an end.*

DAVID: What's this music called?

DIEGO: *Adiós a Cuba* by Ignacio Cervantes . . . a Cuban
who died in 1905. He was once summoned by the
Spanish Captain General who said he liked his work:
'Ignacio Cervantes', he told him, 'we're convinced the

money you collect at your concerts goes to support the insurgents. Get out of here before I'm forced to put you in prison.' (*Changing his tone of voice*) 'I'll go to the United States', he replied, 'where I can continue doing what I do now.' (*Referring to the tea*) Do you want to try it with whisky just for a change? (*He gets another unopened bottle out of the cupboard*)

DAVID: Hey, you've got good supplies. When are you going to pass on your contact?

DIEGO: (*He pours a drop of whisky into each cup, then goes over to the bookcase*) This morning I was reading *Evening Songs*, by Juan Clemente Zenea, 'a prince born of our blood' as Lezama describes him, and I told myself: 'David must read this'. (*Points to the bookcase*) It's right here. Take this one as well, but make sure you cover it. You might get problems.

DAVID: Who said so? I read whatever I want to.

DIEGO: You know what you're doing. I was imprisoned in the UMAP camps for less. And do you know who was there as well? Pablito Milanés.

DAVID: That's past history. And now Pablito is a fantastic revolutionary.

DIEGO: In case you're ever interested in sex you should take this book, a treatise on Marxist sexology which states that 80 per cent of men have a homosexual experience in their life without it affecting their personality.

DAVID: Last time you said it was 60 per cent.

DIEGO: I keep updating it. (*He sits down*) Let's be serious for a moment, when will you bring me some of your writing?

DAVID: I told you they're personal. I won't show them to anybody.

DIEGO: Well, you'll have to make an exception. I want to

be your critic, your agent, your Carmen Balcells. I can
help you get into print, I don't mean here but abroad.
DAVID-*the-secret-policeman* looks interested.

DAVID: Really?

DIEGO: Of course, but first of all I need something to read.
Let's have a change of subject. Have you got a
girlfriend?

DAVID: Yes.

DIEGO: You're a bad liar. Tell me . . . No, forget it.

DAVID: What? Go on.

DIEGO: What do you think about sex?

DAVID: Not more of the same? I don't like talking about
it.

DIEGO: It's very important. Not to say riveting. Say, for
example, the kind of women you fancy. Big bums or
big tits?

DAVID: I prefer women who are revolutionary.

DIEGO: But there are revolutionaries with bums and
revolutionaries without them. Be honest. And have you
ever been to bed with a woman?

DAVID: Of course I have. With several.

DIEGO *doesn't believe a word. Someone knocks on the
door.* DIEGO *looks very fed up.*

DIEGO: I'm not going to open the door!

DAVID: Go on. It's probably from the hospital.

Really upset, DIEGO *gets up and goes out of frame.*
DAVID *strikes a very masculine pose.* DIEGO *comes
back with two envelopes. He passes one on to* DAVID.

DIEGO: You're in luck, my country lad. An invitation to
the ballet.

DAVID: (*Handing it back*) I don't go to the ballet. I don't
like the atmosphere.

DIEGO: (*Offended*) It's not a question of atmosphere or
taste. It's a patriotic duty. Alicia Alonso is dancing

124

Swan Lake, and when that lady gets on stage, she's the
most important event in the city. Here you are.
(He leaves the invitation on DAVID's *legs)*
DAVID: *(He leaves it there)* It will be wasted. Give it to
someone else.

DIEGO *pours tea and whisky into the tea-cups.*
DIEGO: I believe in the power of temptation. Let's drink to
Alicia and to Tchaikovsky. He won't cause you any
problems: he's Russian.
DAVID: To Alicia and 'Haihovski.'
DIEGO: Not 'Haihovski.' Tchaikovsky.
DAVID: Tchai – kov – sky.
They drink.
DIEGO: Now what should we talk about?

47. STUDENT RESIDENCE INT. NIGHT
DAVID *is getting ready to go to bed. The rest of his
companions are asleep. The door opens and in walks*
MIGUEL.
MIGUEL: Have you been with the queer all this time?
DAVID *looks at everyone sleeping. He indicates he should
keep quiet and they go into the corridor.*
MIGUEL: What happened?
DAVID: I met a girl in Central Park, we went to the cinema
. . . I got embroiled.
Now they're in the study area.
MIGUEL: I was going to go to the police. What did you find
out about the exhibition?
DAVID: Very little. Apparently it's all off.
MIGUEL: How come?
DAVID: The director of the gallery took fright. Tomorrow
he's going to negotiate another one at Provincial
Headquarters.
MIGUEL: Let him negotiate. Get him worked up. Tell him

he mustn't give up on any account. Which embassy is helping him?

DAVID *looks as if he never found out.*

MIGUEL: Fuck, DAVID. That's the most important bit. You've got to get that out of him.

DAVID: It's not so easy. Do you want me to put an arm-lock on him?

MIGUEL: If it were me I'd get it out of him. Go back tomorrow!

DAVID: I can't go every day.

MIGUEL: Take him your writing, that's your excuse.

DAVID *doesn't like the suggestion and hides his real feelings with difficulty.*

DAVID: You're taking it too far. We're not policemen or priests.

MIGUEL: You're not weakening now? You know better than anybody that the guy's a queer.

DAVID: But you don't even know him, he's not done you any harm.

MIGUEL: Come on. It really fucks me up. I'm fighting for this country and these queers are free to put on exhibitions and pervert the youth. He should clear off to Miami where he really belongs.

48. STUDENT RESIDENCE: DAVID'S ROOM. INT. NIGHT

DAVID *stretched out on his bed, thoughtful. His face reflects the doubts and tensions he can feel within himself.*

49. THE DEN: SITTING-ROOM. INT. DAY

The room is empty. Knocks at the door.

DIEGO'S VOICE: (*in a bad temper*) Coming!

More insistent knocking. DIEGO *comes into frame and opens up in a bad mood.* NANCY *appears looking radiant. Showing off her bandaged wrists.*

126

NANCY: It's me! (*almost breaking into song*) I'm out of
hospital, I'm off to the beach, and I've come to invite
you to the beach with me.
DIEGO *turns his back on her*. NANCY *walks in after
him.*
DIEGO: You'd better go, I'm seething. How can people be
so stupid and yet you can't say a word?
NANCY: What happened?
DIEGO: Provincial Headquarters rejected Germán's
exhibition! They said no! and that was an end to it!
You can't argue because they give out the orders. I
need a glass of water!
NANCY *at a loss for words.*
DIEGO: They'll only accept *naif* painters, official painters,
or those who say they're modern but don't say or do
anything new, just paint pretty pictures. I asked you to
bring me some water!
NANCY: Don't get annoyed with me. I'm having psychiatric
treatment. Don't get like that.
DIEGO: How do you expect me to act. You tell me! Should
I be laughing. Ha, ha, ha! But don't think I said
nothing.
NANCY: (*Frightened*) What did you say?
DIEGO: What I felt like saying. That there's no freedom
under socialism, that bureaucrats control everything,
that artists can't say what they want . . .
NANCY: Diego, don't say things like that without music on!
(*She runs over to the record-player and puts on a
record*) And all because of those . . .
DIEGO: Those what?
NANCY: (*She points to Germán's pieces*) They depress me,
don't uplift me one bit.
DIEGO: You're just the same! Now whores have turned art
critic! What a wonderful Revolution we've got!

NANCY: Don't call me a whore or I'll throw myself over the balcony! I'm not a whore!

DIEGO: (*In a rage, opens the doors to the balcony.*) Come on, over you go. Let's see who'll pick up the pieces. I'm the only one who'll run after you and I'm not budging.

NANCY *understands that* DIEGO *is really upset. He comes back into the room.*

DIEGO: Art isn't about communication. It's about feeling and thinking. National Radio can communicate.

NANCY: Don't defend Germán so much. He's using you, taking advantage of you. He's as much of a skunk as the rest of them.

DIEGO: (*Not listening to her*) They see attacks and danger on all sides. Nothing's sacred. Any minute now they'll be banning nursery rhymes.

NANCY: Nursery rhymes?

DIEGO: Do you want to hear something really subversive? (*Sings, emphasising the song's 'subversive' content*) 'Paper boat, my faithful friend, SAIL me to the open seas. I want to meet friends from here and OVER THERE . . .'

NANCY: You're impossible, I'll make you a cup of tea.

NANCY *is frightened by lightning.*

NANCY: Holy St Barbara, God protect us! (*Goes out to the balcony and gathers up the clothes drying there. Comes in*) That's the end of the beach for today. The weather's foul.

DIEGO: Don't let them hear you! The weather may be bad, but education and health-care come free.

NANCY *looks on, at a loss for words.*

50. STUDENT RESIDENCE: DAVID'S ROOM. INT.DAY

DAVID *is alone in his room, dressed to go out. He takes a*

wooden suitcase from his cupboard. Puts it on his bed.
The suitcase is locked. Looks for a key which is also
hidden and opens the suitcase. With almost religious
fervour he gets out of the bottom a large envelope from
which he extracts a folder tied with a ribbon. It contains
his literary texts. He looks at it lovingly. Caresses the
covers. Unknots the ribbon and opens it. On the first page
it reads: 'David Alvarez. Another War. Unpublished
stories.' Emotionally, he turns some pages over, caresses
one, read some lines from another. He closes the folder,
puts it away again and decisively returns the suitcase to its
rightful place.

51. OLD HAVANA: STREETS. EXT.DAY
DIEGO *and* GERMÁN *walking along the pavement carrying*
lots of rolls of cardboard. They stop opposite DIEGO's
house. GERMÁN *takes every opportunity to look at the*
beautiful youths they walk past in the street. He
occasionally looks over his shoulder. Snatches of
conversation on the appearance of various men.
DIEGO: You lose one and win another. Where did that guy
     come from, darling?
GERMÁN: From Santiago, honey. That's where I met him.
     As the gallery director knows nothing about the Plastic
     Arts he brought him in as a public relations
     consultant. He'll help us, but, obviously, on the quiet.
DIEGO: (*Wanting to know whether he is homosexual*) And
     is he . . .?
GERMÁN: (*Laughing*) Not officially. But you know what
     this country is like. We're a world power when it
     comes to getting the hots. Look at you, all shacked up
     with a young Communist.
DIEGO: What did he say to you about Mexico?
GERMÁN: That if the exhibition gets through he'll put

pressure on so we can cross the ocean. I made it clear I wouldn't go without you.

DIEGO: I doubt they'll allow that. Even less for us to go together.

GERMÁN: Come on, honey. They need to freshen up their image abroad and what better than a couple of liberal artists who are queens to boot. Repression's out of fashion at the moment. They're using us and we're allowing ourselves to be used. We'll wrap the flag round us, and go like good patriots.

DIEGO: And the rest.

GERMÁN: If you've got a godfather, you're made. Look at old Rhinoceros: in Montreal. We'll get in through Merida, darling, that's as much as to say Puerto Padre, but no matter. Once we're in the land of the Mayas we'll take the world on: two Caribbean termites heading for the top. There'll be no stopping us till we hit El Chopo.

52. THE DEN: SITTING ROOM. INT.DAY

DIEGO, *a camera round his neck, takes the cover off one of the 'provocative series'. Other 'normal' ones have been uncovered and already photographed for the catalogue.*

DIEGO: This is pure dynamite. You must finish the series. It's the strong meat in the exhibition.

GERMÁN *stands behind* DIEGO *looking at the piece unenthusiastically.* DIEGO *puts it into the light.*

GERMÁN: No, I don't like that one, it takes away from me. (*Gets his way and replaces it with another*) Now that highlights my good looks. (*He poses next to the piece and talks while* DIEGO *sets up and takes the photos.*) I've already chosen what to wear at the opening: they'll think I've just come from Paris. (*As if making a casual aside*) My friend came to see me yesterday.

130

DIEGO: (*Breaks off his work*) Oh, really? Did he see the
   pieces?

GERMÁN: He was thrilled by them . . .

DIEGO: (*Pointing to the provocative series.*) These as well?

GERMÁN: He made one or two perceptive little criticisms.
   He thinks it would be best to make a selection.

DIEGO: What?

GERMÁN: Diego, you've got to accept reality. As he says,
   the overall impact is important, not the individual
   pieces.

DIEGO: I guessed as much. I hope you told him it wasn't
   on. Don't even contemplate retreating.

GERMÁN: Don't dig your heels in. Who am I, you tell me?
   Who's heard of me? I'm nobody. I've not even been to
   Guanabacoa. After I've exhibited, had my reviews and
   got my friends abroad, that's when I'll set conditions
   and do whatever I feel like.

DIEGO: Your friend's trying to manipulate us. Go and tell
   him where he can stick his gallery and trip to Mexico.
   Censoring me? at my time of life?

GERMÁN: It's not censorship. He's giving me a chance and
   I'm taking it.

DIEGO: The exhibition stays as it is. If we can't get a
   gallery, we'll put it on in an arcade. Don't argue with
   me. Why don't you clear off, I'm expecting someone
   and don't want them to find you here. (*He takes*
   GERMÁN's *bag and hands it to him*) Off you go.

GERMÁN: (*Very fed up, takes his bag*) Communism's really
   giving you a hard time, duckie. Give my regards to
   your young commissar. (*Exits*)

53. NANCY'S FLAT: BALCONY, LIVING-ROOM. EXT-INT. DAY
NANCY *is dealing with a shopper. There is a variety of*
goods on the table, generally products for women with

131

*famous brand names. There is also a prominent flower
vase stuffed with far too many red flowers. In one corner,
a small altar dedicated to a medium size Santa Barbara-
Changó. Nancy's wrists are bandaged. She is in a good
mood. Background music.*

NANCY: That's really good. You ask your hairdresser.

NEIGHBOUR: Give me a small reduction, please.

NANCY: You always want small reductions. 25 cash!

NEIGHBOUR: All right. The tint, and this face cream. (*Pays
her and leaves*)

NANCY: Next week I'll have tights and children's slippers.
    NANCY *collects up the merchandise. She looks up at
    Santa Barbara as if she can see she's looking
    reproachful. Squares up to her.*

NANCY: Look, it's all good quality. (*Showing her the
    goods*) And I'm the one running risks with the police.
    You only need your candles, I need more than that. If
    they want nice things, they've got to pay for them.
    *She grabs a piece of bread, turns up the volume of the
    music and goes onto the balcony. She leans against the
    parapet and looks casually into the street. Something
    nice catches her eye. She throws the bread away, goes
    into the flat, puts a cloth over her merchandise and in
    front of the mirror very excitedly drags a comb
    through her hair.*

54. DIEGO'S HOUSE: PASSAGEWAY. INT. DAY

DAVID *goes up in the lift. Through the bars he can make
out a man in a passageway carrying half a cow over his
shoulder.* DAVID *stops the lift and goes back down. The
passage looks empty. Someone banging on the floor above.*
DAVID *carries on up. Three drunks banging on the third
floor.*

DRUNK: Hey, brother, collect us when you go down.

DAVID *reaches* DIEGO's *floor. He leaves the lift and shuts it behind him.* NANCY *waits close to the wall, when he walks by she touches him on the back.*

NANCY: Ah!

DAVID *is surprised and turns round.* NANCY, *who has smartened herself up, smiles at him. She's got a red flower in her hair.*

NANCY: I'm shaking all over!

DAVID *is delighted to see* NANCY *as she is to see him.*

DAVID: Are you all right?

NANCY: (*Flirtatiously*) I don't know. You tell me. (*She takes the flower out of her hair and offers it to him*) I wanted to thank you.

DAVID *is delighted by the gesture.* NANCY *looks at him, sizes him up.*

NANCY: Come and have a coffee, or some coconut delight. (*She takes him by the arm and they walk out*) Nobody's coconut is quite like mine.

A QUEEN *who lives in the house, sweeping outside her front-door, has observed the scene, puts her broom down, goes over to* DIEGO's *flat and knocks. In the background,* NANCY *pushes* DAVID *into her room and shuts the door.*

55. NANCY'S APARTMENT: LIVING-ROOM. INT. DAY

DAVID *and* NANCY *in her living-room.*

NANCY: I've got a better idea. I can offer you something I bet you've never tried: whisky.

DAVID *smiles and indicates he hasn't.* NANCY *looks out a bottle identical to* DIEGO's, *with four tots left. She pours out two glasses.*

NANCY: I'm really pleased to be alive. Why should I want to end it all? It was an accident with a knife, when I was peeling potatoes.

133

DAVID: Both wrists?

NANCY: It was a double-bladed knife.

They laugh. DAVID *tries the whisky. It tastes strangely suspicious. He looks at* NANCY *distrustfully.*

NANCY: Is it poisoned? Well, let me drink the poison with you, just like Romeo and Juliet. (*She gulps it down*) DAVID *surreptitiously leaves the glass on a sideboard.*

DAVID: I'm glad you've recovered.

NANCY: How could I not recover with your blood inside me?

DAVID: Diego says . . .

NANCY: Don't believe a word he says. He's a liar.

DAVID: He looked after you properly. He was scared.

NANCY: It suits him for me to be alive. Are you two close friends?

DAVID: I belong to the Communist Youth. He's getting me some books.

NANCY *smiles at the news.*

NANCY: He's got lots of books. So you're a card-carrier. I'll put on some music.

DAVID: Wait, I wanted to ask you. As you belong to the Vigilance Committee . . .

NANCY *is surprised by the turn in the conversation, but hides her feelings.*

DAVID: What kind of person is he? How does he conduct himself politically?

NANCY *sums the situation up quickly. Looks ill at ease.*

NANCY: You ought not to visit him.

DAVID: Why not?

NANCY: It would be better if you didn't.

The door opens and DIEGO *appears behind* NANCY. NANCY *doesn't turn round, but she's seen him, or sensed his presence.*

NANCY: An excellent individual, a marvellous friend, I love him like my own brother . . .

DIEGO: Nancy, have you got my scissors . . .? (*Feigns surprise when he sees* DAVID) Hey, what are you doing here?

NANCY: (*She turns round*) Diego! We were just talking about you, what a coincidence.

DIEGO: Your tea's waiting for you, dear. Come on.

DIEGO *takes advantage of* DAVID'*s embarrassment to take him by the arm and lead him gently towards the passageway.*

DAVID: I'll be seeing you.

NANCY: Thanks for coming to see how I was.

DIEGO: (*To* NANCY, *softly*) You shitty whore, get off my patch.

DAVID *and* DIEGO *leave.* NANCY *watches them walk off looking pleased with herself. She goes in.*

NANCY: (*To* SANTA BARBARA) Did you see the boy's hands. I'm all of a shiver.

56. THE DEN: SITTING-ROOM, INT. DAY

A record on the record-player. A dance by Cervantes.
DAVID *listens intently. His face reflects the deep enjoyment the piece of music is inspiring. A smile comes spontaneously to his lips. When his eyes search out* DIEGO'*s in order to share the emotion he feels, he encounters eyes that are focused on him, quite bewitched.* DAVID *is disturbed by his look, averts his gaze. The music comes to an end.*

DIEGO: It's called *Lost Illusions*. (*He takes the record off*)

DAVID: Why are you that way?

DIEGO: What way?

DAVID: Have you got family?

DIEGO: Well, I didn't come out of thin air, did I?

DAVID: But I bet they don't want to know you now.

DIEGO: Whoever said so? I'm Mum's pride and joy! And my nephews and nieces adore me.

DAVID: But you haven't got a father. He didn't look after you, he deserted the family when you were a kid.

DIEGO: Dad's a saint. I've got his eyes. Thank God because Mum's got a heart of gold and the face of a toad.

DAVID: Then . . . what did happen to you? Why are you . . .?

DIEGO: A queer? Because that's the way I am, I told you! My family knows.

DAVID: They should have taken you to the doctor's when you were a kid . . . it's a hormone problem.

DIEGO: Where did you get that theory, David? It's incredible coming from a university student. You like women. I like men. It's perfectly normal, and doesn't prevent me from being as decent and patriotic as you.

DAVID: Oh, really? You aren't a revolutionary. You're not helping to build our society.

The reproach cuts DIEGO *to the quick.*

DIEGO: Because you people won't let me. I also had my illusions. I went on the literacy campaigns at the age of fourteen, because I insisted when Mum didn't want to let me go. I went to the mountains to pick coffee and decided to study to become a school-teacher and to organise a local theatre group. What happened then? Along came the repression of homosexuals, as if we were responsible for the things that weren't working. You people, if somebody won't say yes to everything or has got different ideas, then you lot want to put that person out of circulation. And that's a fact.

DAVID: And what are the different ideas you defend? Setting up exhibitions with those monstrosities?

DIEGO: And what are you defending? Guard duty, meeting

137

target after target although you think they're completely futile?

DAVID: I'm defending this country and its dignity.

DIEGO: So am I. I don't want the Americans to come or anybody telling us what we have to do. I know only too well what needs defending here. Go out in the street, show a photo of Brezhnev around and everyone will recognise him; but if it's Lezama Lima they'll think he's my father.

DAVID: Do you think anyone can take you and this nonsense seriously? You've read all those books, but you only think about men.

DIEGO: I think about men when it's a time to be thinking about men! Like you and women. And I don't do stupid things. Is this stupid? (*He imitates the mannerisms and tone of voice of a city dude*) 'Tasty, babe.' You people, to try and get me under control, pretend I'm abnormal. But I'm not, I'm not! Laugh at me as much as you like, I don't care, I'll laugh back. I'm part of this country, though you don't like the idea. It's mine and I've got the same right to do things for it as you have, so stuff that, you shit-bag.
Someone knocking at the door. DIEGO, *in a rage, goes to answer.*

DIEGO: (*He shouts out*) I don't need the scissors now!
He stands with his back to the door. DAVID *looks at him in dismay. He is impressed by the vehemence of* DIEGO's *self-defence. After a moment, the latter opens the door without turning round.*

DIEGO: I'd like you to leave . . .
DAVID *leaves silently.* DIEGO *closes the door and goes over to the Virgin. His eyes are full of tears. He recovers slightly.*

DIEGO: (*To the Virgin*) If you don't want to be burnt, get him back here.

57. GRAN TEATRO: ARCADE & ENTRANCE. EXT-INT DAY

Lots of people in the foyer to the Gran Teatro. Among the crowd, bejewelled ladies, gentlemen with aristocratic airs, ethereal young women, finicky young men, extremely old old ladies, gossiping like old acquaintances: the real image of bourgeois decadence in the eyes of MIGUEL *and* DAVID *who look on from a distance. Several of the opera buffs are wearing flowers.*

MIGUEL: All this lot will be off to Miami at the first opportunity. Not a single revolutionary among them. DAVID *acts rather reserved, obviously he's there because he didn't have any choice in the matter. Suddenly, despite himself, his face goes tense.* MIGUEL *looks in the same direction.* DIEGO *makes his triumphal entry, accompanied by* GERMÁN *and a* GRANDE DAME *who is treated like a countess. Everybody is dressed in evening dress:* DIEGO *is in black and* GERMÁN *wears a red reversible jacket. The trio's arrival causes a stir.* MIGUEL *needs no more to tell him these are the people he is waiting for.*

MIGUEL: Which are they?

DAVID (*hesitantly*): The ones over there.

MIGUEL: (*Hesitantly*) Is the other fellow the sculptor? You can see they're a couple of shits from a mile off. DIEGO *and his retinue walk into the theatre lobby. At a particular moment,* DIEGO *looks round searching out* DAVID. *He can't see him.*

DAVID and MIGUEL *hand over their invitations. The* DOORMAN *looks them up and down and, rather contemptuously, holds them back and checks their invitations carefully.*

MIGUEL: Anything wrong, my friend? If so, do let me know. *The* DOORMAN *lets them in.*

DIEGO *and* GERMÁN *surrounded by* EPHEBES, *two or*

three QUEENS, DAMES *and other characters, chatting
and laughing. Every so often* DIEGO *looks round.*
GERMÁN *looks out of frame, sees someone, and digs*
DIEGO *in the ribs.*
(To DIEGO) There's our man.
DIEGO *looks.* GERMÁN'S FRIEND, *a provincial nouveau
riche who has fallen on his feet in the capital, is
talking to other official personages. He's well-built,
looks like a black belt.*
DIEGO: That fellow? He looks as if he knows as much
about the plastic arts as I know about pancakes.
GERMÁN *smiles at his* FRIEND, *who responds discreetly
from a distance.*
GERMÁN: Don't criticise him. He's OK.
DIEGO: The people in front of him are official types and
the ones behind are liberals and they're the worst.
A BEAUTIFUL ADOLESCENT *passes by and is recognised
by* GERMÁN.
GERMÁN: The only thing that matters is for us to be
despatched to Mexico, darling. Excusez-moi. (*He goes
after the Adolescent.*)
MIGUEL *and* DAVID. MIGUEL *looks out of frame.*
MIGUEL: Wait for me here. (*He goes off*)
DAVID *sees* DIEGO *and hides. He picks up a programme
and starts reading.*

58. GRAN TEATRO: LAVATORIES. INT. DAY
MIGUEL *goes into the lavatories; the* BEAUTIFUL
ADOLESCENT *is just leaving.* GERMÁN *is in front of the
mirror, tidying his hair. He sees* MIGUEL, *who in turn looks
at him and goes over to the urinals.* GERMÁN *looks at him
again,* MIGUEL *briefly turns his head round.* GERMÁN *walks
over to the urinals.* MIGUEL *looks at him and gives a
neutral smile, opens his fly wider as if to urinate more*

141

comfortably. GERMÁN *looks.* MIGUEL *lets him have a good look, moves slightly away from the urinal and turns towards* GERMÁN, *almost casually.* GERMÁN *looks around, sees that nobody is there, looks at* MIGUEL, *who is now looking perplexed, and goes over. After a moment's hesitation he holds his hand out towards* MIGUEL'*s cock;* MIGUEL *grabs his hand violently.*

MIGUEL: What were you going to do? You're a pansy. Let's go to the manager's office.

GERMÁN: (*Very frightened*) No, please, it was a mistake. I wasn't going to do anything.

    MIGUEL *twists his arm, immobilises him.*

MIGUEL: You weren't going to do anything? Let's go to the police.

GERMÁN: (*Terrified*) No, I'll give you whatever you want. I'll give you my money, my chain. Anything to avoid a scene.

MIGUEL: (*Lets him go*) Let's have a look at your chain.

GERMÁN: (*Gives his chain*) I never do things like that.

MIGUEL: Now your money.

GERMÁN: (*Gives him his wallet*) All right. Please let me go now.

MIGUEL: (*Goes through his wallet, takes money out*) Are you trying to bribe me?

GERMÁN: (*In a blind panic*) No. I'm not. Nothing of the kind. God, please help me.

MIGUEL: What have you got in your bag?

GERMÁN: Nothing, bits and pieces.

MIGUEL: I bet you've got some pornography. Let me have a look.

    Voices of people coming in. MIGUEL *turns round.* GERMÁN *snatches his chain and runs off, pushing the people who are coming in.* MIGUEL *recovers himself, but, with his flies still open, his position is ambiguous.*

The people coming in look at him rather suspiciously.
MIGUEL, *not allowing himself to be intimidated, does*
up his flies, looks at GERMÁN's *wallet and puts it away*
with a smirk of satisfaction.

59. GRAN TEATRO: LOBBY. INT. DAY
DAVID *reading the programme. When he looks up he is*
eyeball to eyeball with DIEGO *who is just walking though.*
They are both surprised. DIEGO *recovers straightaway,*
bends down to tie up a shoelace and speaks between
gritted teeth.
DIEGO: Please come back. I'm sorry about the other day.
    Promise me you'll come.
    DAVID *moves away without replying. A warning-bell*
    rings. MIGUEL *joins* DAVID.
MIGUEL: When we get out of here, I'll take you out for a
    restaurant meal.

60. GRAN TEATRO: AUDITORIUM. INT.
DAVID *and* MIGUEL *take their seats. The second bell rings.*
DAVID *looks around. But he isn't looking for* DIEGO. *He is*
feasting his eyes on the decor, the lights, the spectators, the
balconies. He spots DIEGO *and retinue in one of the main*
boxes.
MIGUEL *also looks around, to no avail.*
DIEGO *sees* DAVID. *Suddenly,* GERMÁN, *quite overwhelmed,*
comes in, collapses on the seat next to him.
GERMÁN: Sweetie, what a close shave. I was wrong-footed
    by a policeman in the toilet.
DIEGO: In here?
GERMÁN: In here. No respect anymore not even for the
    Holy See. (*He pulls up one trouser-leg, takes a wallet*
    out and puts it in his jacket pocket) Just as well I had
    my buggers' wallet on. I lost twenty pesos. (*He*

144

changes his appearance slightly, puts sequins on, turns
his reversible jacket inside out. etc.)
The lights go out. The curtain goes up. The stage is
immediately filled with white ballerinas. DAVID *looks*
on attentively. MIGUEL *remains as stiff as cardboard at*
his side. The performance starts.
At every moment, DIEGO *observes* DAVID. *The latter is*
enjoying the ballet. Shots of the dancing. Suddenly, the
audience near DAVID *and* MIGUEL *and the whole*
audience stand up, start applauding and shouting
'Bravo! bravoo!, bravoo! DAVID *and* MIGUEL *also get*
up and applaud not knowing why they're applauding.
MIGUEL *looks one way and another.*

MIGUEL: Has Fidel just arrived?

ALICIA ALONSO *slips in on points from one side of the*
stage as if she isn't touching the ground. The applause
intensifies. ALICIA *responds: she goes to the front of*
the stage and bows, which stirs the audience up even
more. DAVID *applauds enthusiastically.* MIGUEL *elbows*
him in the ribs.

MIGUEL: Don't applaud.

DAVID: It's Alicia Alonso.

MIGUEL: So what? They're all queers.

DAVID: Alicia is a Party member.

MIGUEL *looks at him incredulously.*

DAVID: It's true.

Reluctantly MIGUEL *applauds. On stage Alicia starts*
dancing again.
The ballet. The audience is silent and attentive,
holding its breath. DAVID *is taken aback and can't take*
his eyes off ALICIA. *The more she dances, the more he*
looks at her, and forgets everybody else, as if he were
the only person in the theatre and ALICIA *were only*
dancing for him. MIGUEL *has fallen asleep.*

Out of the corner of his eye DIEGO *observes* DAVID
enjoying himself. GERMÁN *notices and wants to know
who he is looking at. He takes the* GRANDE DAME's
opera glasses, but DIEGO *complains he's being frivolous
and takes the glasses away from him.* GERMÁN *doesn't
get to see* DAVID *or* MIGUEL.
DAVID *is following the ballet. In his eyes, the stage
starts to seem enchanted, an unreality matching his
dazzled bewilderment and the dancers become
luminous, fade, turn in on themselves, dance through
the air, float, fly . . .
Suddenly, in the midst of deafening chords from the
orchestra, the* MAGICIAN *makes his surprise
appearance, leaping across the stage, waving his very
long arms most threateningly.* DAVID *is frightened and*
MIGUEL *wakes up.*

MIGUEL: What happened?

DAVID, *concentrating on the stage, makes no response.
The* MAGICIAN *takes hold of* ALICIA ALONSO, *takes her
away from the* PRINCE, *carries her off to the dismay of
both, of the audience and of* DAVID.
*The audience bursts into spectacular applause, verging
on hysteria.* MIGUEL *is appalled and looks round, looks
at* DAVID. *He is applauding enthusiastically.*

61. THE DEN: SITTING-ROOM. INT. DAY

DIEGO *and* GERMÁN *in a heated argument.* DIEGO *snatches
away a sculpture that* GERMÁN *is trying to put to one side,
and restores it to the group.*

DIEGO: You're not removing a single one. Let them learn
to respect the freedom of the artist.

GERMÁN: Be reasonable! If not, I won't be off to Mexico!

DIEGO: Don't go! Are you an artist or a tourist?

GERMÁN: I'm more of an artist than you are.

DIEGO: Act like one then. Suffer. Respect and defend your
work. Every piece is going to be included.

GERMÁN: I'm not arguing anymore . . .

*He goes over to the sculptures and starts to destroy
what's at the centre of the row. DIEGO tries to prevent
him. They get locked in struggle.*

62. DIEGO'S HOUSE: PASSAGEWAY. INT. DAY

*The passageway. DIEGO's door opens and GERMÁN is
violently ejected. Fragments of his scuptures, his bag,
flowers and things rain down on him. The neighbours peer
out and enjoy the row. NANCY looks out as well.*

A VOICE: Somebody's knocked the vase of pansies over!

GERMÁN *holds tight to his bag and runs to the stairs.*
DIEGO *goes out into the passageway.*

GERMÁN: May St Peter bless the man with the gift from
God. If you were going on the trip, you wouldn't be so
fussy!

NANCY *looks on anxiously from the doorway to her
flat.*

63. THE DEN: SITTING-ROOM. INT. DAY

DIEGO *loses his temper. He looks at the damage wrought
by* GERMÁN *and gets even more furious. He crashes his
typewriter down on his worktable, puts some music on
(almost a military march) and sits down at the typewriter.*

DIEGO: They'll learn. And all the other third-raters with
him.

*He sweeps the table clean with a flourish of the hand, puts
a sheet of paper in his typewriter and starts typing like a
madman. The open balcony is his only source of light.*

64. STUDENT RESIDENCE: DAVID'S ROOM. INT. DAY

DAVID's *alone in his room, lying on his bed. He's looking for*

*a favourite programme on a small portable radio. As he
tunes in, he hears a fragment of* Swan Lake. *He goes back to
that station: they are broadcasting a commentary on a
performance of the ballet, accompanied by musical excerpts.*
DAVID *is lost in his memories. He gets up, gets down the
suitcase containing his literary efforts, opens it, takes out an
exercise book. He becomes emotional as he did on a
previous occasion, hesitates. He comes to a decision: takes
out the exercise book and returns the case to its place.*

65. THE DEN: SITTING-ROOM. INT. EVENING
DIEGO, *wearing a pince-nez, seated at his work-table,
almost in darkness, writing furiously. There are papers
everywhere. When someone knocks at the door his hands
remain in mid-air, he stares at the door like some evil
ogre. The door is half ajar and* DAVID *peers in.* DIEGO's
face is transformed, as if by magic.
DIEGO: (*Cheerfully*) DAVID!
DAVID: (*Rather curtly*) Hello. How are you?
　　They look at each other slightly awkwardly. DIEGO
　　stares at the folder DAVID *is carrying.*
DIEGO: What's that? I don't believe it. Your writing? (*He
　　gets up and walks over to him*)
DAVID: (*Stepping back*) Look, these are my first attempts
　　. . . not my most recent efforts . . . They need
　　correcting. This isn't even my final version. I've got
　　better things but I couldn't find them.
DIEGO: Hand them over then.
DAVID: Don't show them to anybody.
DIEGO: I promise.
DAVID *offers him the folder, but still hangs back.*
DAVID: You may find some spelling mistakes, a girlfriend
　　typed them up for me.
　　DIEGO *snatches the folder from him.*

148

DIEGO: Here lies the truth! The work itself. Nothing else matters. I'll read it this evening and we can talk about it tomorrow. We'll see if you deserve the Lezaman lunch I promised you.

DAVID: I brought your books back. (*Gets them out of his rucksack*)

DIEGO: Did Juan Clemente Zenea make an impact?

DAVID: Who'd have thought someone was writing like that in nineteenth-century Cuba?

DIEGO: We've still a long way to go: praising his virtues and understanding the weaknesses. (*He picks up a pile of books*) I put these to one side for you, with a real jewel: poems by Dulce María Loynaz given to me by her own fair hand.

DAVID: Is the lady still alive?

DIEGO: Alive and kicking, waiting for the storm to pass. One day I'll take you to meet her. The china cups . . .

DAVID: From Sèvres.

DIEGO: They're a present from her. Of course, she's very up in arms. She lent her house for a film shoot and I think they messed everything up. (*The suggestion is they robbed her*) I feel partly to blame: she consulted me and I told her Titón, the director, is a genius. Which is true: him and Humberto Solas. The rest are Alfredo Guevara's creations. (*He goes in the direction of the kitchen*)

DAVID *notices traces of the fight with* GERMÁN. *He goes to the worktable.*

DAVID: And what happened here?

He doesn't get a reply. He peers at the letter DIEGO *is writing.* DIEGO *comes in, rushes over to* DAVID *and takes the sheet of paper from him.*

DIEGO: Don't be so rude, don't do that sort of thing. Wait to be given things, as I did.

DAVID: I'm sorry. What is it?

DIEGO: A letter to the director of a gallery, copied to everybody.

DAVID looks interested. DIEGO picks up the rest of the writing-paper and puts them safely out of reach of DAVID's inquisitive gaze.

DAVID: What's it all about?

DIEGO: About telling a few home truths it was time someone let them in on.

DAVID: Have they rejected your friend's exhibition again?

DIEGO: Worse than that: they've bought it.

DAVID: Well, I can tell you I'm really pleased. That exhibition was always going to be bad news.

DIEGO: Thank you. But I can assure you they'll not feel so perky when they get this.

DAVID: What have you said to them?

DIEGO: What needed saying. That they should respect artists. Propaganda and art are not at all the same thing. If they don't want to think, they've got television, newspapers and everything else.

DAVID: Are you going to send that letter?

DIEGO: Someone's got to tell them, right?

DAVID: But why does it have to be you?

DIEGO: Why not me? I know why. Oh, dearie, thank God intellectual thought isn't distributed via the workplace and neighbourhood meetings.

DAVID: You'll get a load of trouble.

DIEGO: That's my problem! Let's have a drink, I've gone completely light-headed.

(He gets a bottle of whisky from the cupboard – it's always a new one)

DAVID: Can't you see you're all mixed up? You want to post letters and drink whisky? You don't buy that from the cornershop. Come on, where do you get it? Who gives it to you?

DIEGO: (*Upset*) I can't say.

DAVID: Yes, you can!

DIEGO: It's a secret.

DAVID: Well, it does me no good to visit a house with so many secrets. Give me back my stories. I'm off.

DIEGO: Don't get like that. You're quite wrong. The bureaucrats have to be put firmly in their place, David. If not, they'll ruin everything, even the good things about the Revolution.

DAVID: How do you explain that you've always got whisky? This place is full of propaganda, magazines, photos, the whole lot. You do business with foreigners. Where do you get your whisky from? Tell me or I'm off!

DIEGO: (*Lowers his head*) It is not whisky!

DAVID: Isn't it? What is it? A 'taste' of whisky?

DIEGO: It's rum. It's always the same bottle. I wrap it up like that because . . . you don't, but the other youths go mad when they see foreign drink.

DAVID: I wasn't born yesterday. I can see through it when you open them.

DIEGO: It's a trick . . . I do it with my mouth.

He shows him: pretends to open the 'sealed' bottle, imitating the noise with his mouth. DAVID *is amazed.* DIEGO *takes a bottle of rum out of the cupboard. Shows it to him.*

DIEGO: Cheap rum, with root of ginger.

DAVID: (*Confused*) But . . . you can't do that. It's not right.

DIEGO: Why are you all so superficial . . .

DAVID *can't get over it.*

66. SCHOOL OF POLITICAL SCIENCES: LECTURE THEATRE, CORRIDORS. INT. DAY

DAVID *in the lecture theatre not paying attention to the lecturer, distracted, worried. The class comes to an end,* DAVID *picks his things up and leaves with everyone else, he's carrying one of* DIEGO'*s book. Near the stairs, he can see* MIGUEL *on the ground floor and turns back to avoid being seen by him.*

MIGUEL *sees* DAVID, *leaves the friends he's talking to and goes upstairs to look for him. He roams the corridors, looks in a toilet, and a lecture theatre. He gives up, somewhat surprised.*

When MIGUEL *has disappeared, the door to a lecture theatre opens and* DAVID *emerges, still cautiously.* MIGUEL *catches him at the bottom of the stairs.*

MIGUEL: Hey, poet, it's really difficult catching up with you these days. (*He puts an arm round his shoulders*) Listen to what I've found out: the exhibition can be interpreted as ideological propaganda. And foreigners are helping him, he'll get 10 to 15 years inside at the very least.

DAVID: (*Stops*) Are you crazy?

MIGUEL: What's up with you?

DAVID: I'm not going to waste any more time on that poor devil. Let him be. Besides they've given up on the exhibition.

MIGUEL: Poor devil? (*He snatches the book he is holding*) What are you reading now?

DAVID *recovers his book equally roughly.*

DAVID: Whatever I feel like.

MIGUEL: Poetry. Has that queer won you over?

DAVID: Nobody wins me over. I win my own battles.
(*Turns his back on him and leaves*)
MIGUEL *watches him leave.*

153

67. STREET: A POST BOX. EXT. DAY

A post box. DIEGO *appears, stops in front of the post box. People pass either side of him. Someone posts a letter and walks on.* DIEGO *takes out several envelopes. He is indecisive. It's a moment of truth for him. He looks in the direction of a hoarding where you can read the phrase by* MARTÍ *which we have already seen in the city:* 'The frail should be patient, onward the strong; this is a task for the strong'. DIEGO *makes his mind up: posts his letters.*

68. THE DEN: SITTING-ROOM. EXT. DAY

It's five to five by the clock on the wall. DIEGO *is waiting anxiously for* DAVID, *runs from one side to another arranging the scenario. He gets a bottle of wine from the fridge, places it by two delicate wine glasses on a tray and hides the lot behind the bureau. He checks the bookcase where he has pulled out some books so he can easily lay his hands on them. He sits at his worktable. Knocking at the door. He pretends he is working.*

DIEGO'S VOICE: Oui. Entrez-vous, s'il vous plaît. La porte est ouverte.

> DAVID *walks in,* DIEGO *looks at him over his pince-nez.*

DIEGO: A very good afternoon to you, my dear David Alvarovitch. How are things on the *kolschov*?

DAVID: (*On his guard*) Why did you say that?

DIEGO: (*He places the exercise-book on the table*) Because of this!

> DAVID *can see that it's his exercise-book.* DIEGO's *tone doesn't augur at all well.*

DAVID: Aren't they any good?

DIEGO: This isn't literature! It's lifeless, pure sloganising!

> DAVID *feels he's lost both heaven and earth.*

DIEGO: All you forgot was to write *mujhik* instead of

154

peasant. Too much reading Progress Books and the Revolutionary Press, my darling.

DAVID: Leave the Soviet Union in peace. The Soviet Union saved humanity from fascism.

DIEGO: Bolshoi and amen. But, honey, your Spanish sounds as if it's been translated from Russian by an exile from the Spanish Civil War.

DAVID: Didn't you even like . . . the one about the workers going on strike?

DIEGO: That was the worst one. Who told you that the 1933 Revolution took place in 25? I marked in red all the spelling and punctuation mistakes made by your typist girlfriend, and the pages look as if they've got chicken pox. (*He hands over the exercise book*)
DAVID, *bewildered, flicks through it as he sits down.*
DIEGO *lets him suffer for a moment.*

DIEGO: But don't get down-hearted, dearie. You've got talent! There's gold among the dross.
DAVID *looks at him with hope renewed.*

DAVID: Really?

DIEGO: Of course. And you've come to just the right teacher. That's if you'll accept me as a tutor.

DAVID: On one condition. That you forget the exhibition and don't send that letter.

DIEGO: It's a deal. Bye-bye, exhibition.
He gets up and takes the tray with the bottle of wine and glasses from its hiding-place. Goes over to the bookcase.

DIEGO: (*Gathers up the books he'd previously selected*)
First of all, I'll clear out your system: Cuban literature and art in the morning, and Cuban literature and art in the afternoon. And be prepared to walk around Havana: we live in one of the most beautiful cities in the world and you're in time to gaze at some of its

155

wonders before your people allow them to collapse
and be covered in shit.

DAVID: Diego, don't be unfair. There's lots to do and it's a
small country. Nancy went to hospital and it didn't
cost her anything, just remember that. A hundred
dollars doesn't repair a city.

DIEGO: They're allowing it to fall into ruins, don't try to
deny it! They couldn't care less.

DAVID: Some of us care. You and I care.

DIEGO: And what's worse: people are giving up on their
love for the city. And if people stop loving and needing
what is beautiful, what hope is there? We'll end up
thinking that being Cuban is getting drunk and picking
a quarrel just for the sake of it. Let's change the
subject. (*He takes over his pile of books and drops
them into* DAVID's *lap*) There you are for starters. (*He
goes over to the table, pours out the drinks, offers*
DAVID *one*) 'Now we're going into battle . . . Forward
march!'

The scene ends on DAVID *and his huge pile of books.*

69. DAVID'S APPRENTICESHIP

DAVID *walks around the Plaza Vieja, an area that is being
intensively restored. You can see very beautiful seventeenth
to nineteenth-century buildings that have been completely
refurbished enabling one to admire the beauty and
magnificence of the square. By their side are others
undergoing restoration; workers and specialists beavering
away. Other buildings, although they preserve part of their
façades, are beyond repair.* DAVID *walks into some of the
restored courtyards, the beauty of which intensifies the
pain caused by interiors that are now beyond repair.* DAVID
*feels really torn when confronted with what has been lost.
Then he walks along a street staring at people, looking*

156

into houses and yards through windows and open doors.
He can see poverty and overcrowding (poverty, not
starvation). But people look basically cheerful and are
reasonably dressed; they look, as Hemingway would say,
undefeated, with music playing everywhere, getting on
together in an undisciplined bustle in the street as is the
wont of the people of Havana. Ordinary people deserving
a better material and spiritual life.
Through a brief sequence of images we witness the
beginning of DAVID's *apprenticeship under* DIEGO's
guidance, which also strengthens their friendship. We can
see DAVID *reading (in the National Library, travelling by*
bus, in John Donne's armchair); looking at paintings in the
National Museum; typing on DIEGO's *typewriter; getting*
books off the bookshelf; putting a record on the record-
player; opening the refrigerator, drinking a glass of milk
and kicking it shut; arguing with DIEGO, *eating spaghetti*
with him; DIEGO *checking and correcting sheets of paper*
given him by DAVID. *Everything to a background of Cuban*
music. From now on DAVID *still dresses cheaply but with*
slightly more style. His hair also looks more attractive.

70. STUDENT RESIDENCE: WAY IN. EXT. DAY
DAVID *comes out of the building.* A FRIEND *points out that*
someone is looking for him. DAVID *looks to where his*
friend is pointing. He sees VIVIAN.

71. THE MALECÓN. EXT. DAY
VIVIAN *and* DAVID *walk silently along the Malecón. He*
acts with cold but friendly reserve.
VIVIAN: Perhaps I shouldn't have come to say goodbye to
   you. I'm leaving tomorrow and I didn't want to leave
   thinking you are still angry with me.
   They walk on saying nothing.

VIVIAN: If you want you can write to me.

DAVID *stops.*

DAVID: I've got classes now, I can't walk any further. (*They look at each other*) Thanks for coming. I hope everything turns out fine.

VIVIAN: Don't be so hard on me, David. I'm really sorry. It's not my fault.

DAVID *forces a smile.*

DAVID: I know. Don't worry. Goodbye. (*He goes out of frame*)

VIVIAN *watches him walk off into the distance.*

VIVIAN: Good luck, David.

72. THE DEN: SITTING ROOM. INT. DAY

Music. NANCY *comes in, stops dead, interested by what she can see:* DAVID *who, shirtless and shoeless, surrounded by the light from the balcony, is sitting on the ground next to John Donne's armchair, sad and distracted, a glass of rum in one hand and the bottle of 'whisky' by his side.*

NANCY's *gaze turns to real female fascination. She's about to say something to him when* DIEGO *calls her in from the kitchen door, telling her to leave him alone. Intrigued,* NANCY *goes into the kitchen.*

NANCY: What's up with him?

DIEGO: He's been like that for hours. He came in and asked for drink. Usually he doesn't even want water.

NANCY *peers round, looks at* DAVID *again, who at that moment is pouring himself a stiff glass of rum that he gulps down. She speaks with real feeling.*

NANCY: He's so good-looking, Diego.

DIEGO *looks at her rather oddly, as if he has something on his mind.*

NANCY: Why look at me like that? Is it a sin to glory in him?

158

DIEGO: I've been wanting to ask you a favour for days.
(*He can't bring himself to do so*)
NANCY: Go on.
They look at each other suspiciously.
DIEGO: (*Turns away*) Get me a bottle of whisky.
NANCY *knows that wasn't what* DIEGO *was going to ask her. She empties out her bag, from which several packets of tights and children's slippers emerge. She pokes at the bottom and takes out a roll of notes.*
NANCY: I sold your watch. I couldn't get much for it.
DIEGO: Every little helps.
NANCY: The whole lot comes to 300 dollars. Count it, I like things straight, particularly when dollars are involved.
DIEGO *tells her to lower her voice, reminds her of* DAVID's *presence, and counts out the money.*
DIEGO: Nancy, how can I thank you.
NANCY: But I can't sell anything else for the moment. It's really bad on the street. How did your meeting go?
DIEGO: (*Depressed*) They didn't even let me speak. They sacked me. I can't work in anything to do with culture.
NANCY *looks at him sorrowfully*
NANCY: What are you going to do?
DIEGO: I'm going to surprise them! I've got my interview at the Embassy.
NANCY: (*Really happy*) That's great! (*In a quite different tone of voice*) Oh, Diego!
Both start to look serious and sad, for both know what that really means. DIEGO *immediately pulls himself together.*
DIEGO: (*Returning part of the money*) Keep it in your place, they might search mine.
NANCY: Are things that bad?

159

DIEGO: I'm at their mercy. Those letters mean they can accuse me of whatever they want. (*Referring to the money in his hand*) I want to buy David a present with this money.

NANCY: Are you crazy?

DIEGO: I want him to dress elegantly for the Lezama Lima lunch.

NANCY: A Lezama Lima lunch will set you back one hundred dollars. You need that money.

DIEGO: A twenty-year-old youth who's never worn a suit. He deserves one. He's worked hard and he's got talent.

NANCY: You think everyone's got talent. Take that cockroach Germán who's really fucked you up.

DIEGO: He was talented. But to be an artist, talent isn't enough, at least in this country. (*Referring to* DAVID) He mustn't know anything, not a whisper. I'll tell him I asked for some leave.

NANCY: Diego, it's dangerous having that boy around so much. Remember he's a Young Communist and all that. He'll soon cotton on.

DIEGO: You seem to be very keen on me getting rid of him.

NANCY: (*Rather embarrassed*) Why should that be?

DIEGO: So you can take him over. You think I don't notice the way you look at him.

NANCY: Spare me that, I'm off. If you get caught, it's your problem.

DIEGO: The favour I was going to ask you involves him.
NANCY *gets on the defensive.*

DIEGO: He's never been with a woman. That's what's the matter with him.

NANCY: So what?

DIEGO: Why don't you initiate him?
NANCY's *violent reaction surprises* DIEGO

NANCY: You're the last person I'd have expected to come

out with such a thing. Who do you think I am? (*She picks her things up in order to leave*)

DIEGO: Wait a minute, you didn't hear me right.

NANCY: I heard you perfectly well. I'm no whore, get that! *She leaves.* DIEGO *goes after her. They cross the living-room.*

DIEGO: Let me explain. I didn't mean that.

NANCY: No need to explain anything. Count me out. Get yourself another hunk of meat!
She slams the door behind her. DIEGO *goes after her, but* DAVID, *who has tried to get up, slips and falls noisily to the floor.* DIEGO *rushes to help him.*

73. NANCY'S FLAT. INT. DAY

NANCY *comes in in a rage. She looks for a rope and starts preparing to hang herself.*

NANCY: And he says he's a friend of mine. I hope they find him out and put him in prison. (*To Santa Barbara*) Yours truly won't be going to visit him.
(*She throws the rope over a beam in the ceiling. Checks that it holds firm*) What can he have told the boy about me. (*She puts the rope around her neck, but suddenly changes her mind. Looks defiantly at Santa Barbara*) No, dear. Can't you think of anything else to do? I like the lad, but, so what? Why should I be his whore? (*She takes the rope from around her neck and throws it on the floor*)

74. THE DEN: SITTING-ROOM. INT. NIGHT

DIEGO *comes over to* DAVID's *side with a cup of coffee; he's lying on the sofa in a deep sleep. He's not wearing a shirt, his arms are folded over his head and his trouser-fly is open. You can see the top of his pubic hair.* DIEGO *gazes at him. Puts the cup down, sits on the edge of the sofa,*

161

taps him gently on the cheek, to find out how deeply he is
sleeping rather than to wake him up. DAVID *doesn't even*
stir. Then DIEGO *gazes at him in earnest: at his face, his*
stomach, at what's visible around the unzipped trousers;
once again, his face, chest and stomach. Feels an
irresistible desire to touch him. His hand moves towards
DAVID's *body. He holds back. His face reflects the struggle*
between the desire to touch him and the wish to control
himself. In the end, he overcomes the urge. He picks up a
blanket which is at hand and covers him over. Lifts up his
feet, puts cushions round him, makes him as comfortable
as possible. Goes out of frame.

75. NANCY'S FLAT. INT. NIGHT
NANCY, *naked, kneeling on the floor, saying the prayer of*
the Lonely Soul. Next to her, a candle on a saucer, the
only light in the room. She puts her hands in a basin full
of water, flowers and petals which is in front of her and
pours the water over her body.
NANCY: 'Sad, lonely Soul, enter the heart of David Alvarez;
    let no woman black, white, Chinese or mulatto go
    with him; with my second prayer I measure him, with
    my third I tie him, I drink the blood of his heart and
    snatch him from his heart; make him come to my feet
    like our Lord Jesus Christ surrendering at the feet of
    Pontius Pilate.'

76. THE DEN: SITTING-ROOM. INT. DAY
The morning light creeps in through the balcony. DAVID *is*
asleep on the sofa. NANCY *unlocks the door and comes*
secretively in. She looks at DIEGO's *Virgin.*
NANCY: Help me control him, and don't go gossiping to
    the other girl.
    She asks permission and takes one of the sunflowers.

162

She goes over to DAVID *and contemplates him at her leisure. She strokes him with the flower until he wakes up. Startled,* DAVID *sits up on the sofa, not sure where he is. Although he's wearing his trousers, he immediately pulls the blanket over his crotch.*

DAVID: What am I doing here?

NANCY: You're not here. It's a dream.

DAVID *remembers what the situation is.*

DAVID: What's the time?

NANCY: Midday, lazybones.

DAVID: And what about Diego?

NANCY: Don't get Diego mixed up in this dream. He had to go out. He asked me to give you some lunch and take you for a walk.

DAVID: Take me out then.

NANCY *gives a smile of delight.*

77. AN EMBASSY TERRACE. EXT. DAY
The shot is taken from quite a distance, the patio is in the foreground and the main entrance in the background. In the doorway, DIPLOMAT 1 *sits up in his armchair where he's reading the newspaper and cheerfully greets* DIEGO, *who arrives accompanied by* DIPLOMAT 2. *He invites him to sit down. They start a friendly conversation.*

78. AN EMBASSY GARDEN. EXT. DAY
DIEGO *and* DIPLOMAT 2 *leave the house and walk across the garden. It is obvious they are friends. The* DIPLOMAT *accompanies* DIEGO *to the door to the garden, where he says a friendly goodbye and gives him encouraging slaps on the back.* DIEGO *is clearly pleased.*

NOTE: *at no time is the embassy identified. Appearances indicate that it is an unidentified country in Western Europe.*

79. THE MALECÓN: A STREET IN OLD HAVANA. EXT. DAY

NANCY, *accompanied by* DAVID, *buys flowers.* DAVID *goes as if to pay, but she won't let him. They start walking.*

NANCY: They're pretty, aren't they?

DAVID: Lovely.

NANCY: When I'm happy I buy flowers. When I'm sad as well. I'm always giving myself flowers. (*Suddenly*) Shall we go to the Malecón? (*She holds his hand and they quicken their pace*)

80. THE AVENIDA DEL PUERTO: THE MALECÓN. EXT. DAY

DAVID *and* NANCY *walking along the sea front.*

DAVID: Tell me about yourself.

NANCY: About myself? Why do you want to find out about me, dear?

DAVID: About your family, anything . . .

NANCY: They live in Cabaiguán. I live all by myself. Let's sit down over there.

She points to a section of the wall. She walks on and sits down. DAVID *catches her up.*

NANCY: The sea is beautiful, isn't it? Give me your hand, I want to read your palm. (DAVID *holds out his hand*)

NANCY: Your right hand.

DAVID: That is my right hand.

NANCY: Really? (*She reads it*) Your life is on the brink of a great love affair. One love comes to an end and another starts suddenly, just like that.

DAVID: (*Amused*) When is your birthday?

NANCY: I'm Aries. An Aries woman and a Virgo man get on really well, you know.

DAVID: (*Smiling*) Where do you work?

NANCY: (*Suddenly*) Look there's the ferry! Let's go to Regla! *Hand in hand they run towards the ferry. They get on at the last moment. One take gives a view of*

*Casablanca on the other side of the bay, with the
figure of Christ towering in the sky.*

81. THE FERRY. INT. DAY

DAVID *and* NANCY *sit next to the window. She looks out
and he looks at her. She knows he's looking at her. Finally
she looks at him.*

NANCY: Look at the view.

> DAVID *smiles and continues to look at her. She returns
> his look.*

DAVID: Don't you want to know what I think about love?

> DAVID *nods his head gently.* NANCY *gets circumspect.*

NANCY: I'm far too old for you.

DAVID: Far too old for what?

> NANCY *feels she's been caught on the hop*

82. A NIGHT CLUB. INT. NIGHT

NANCY *and* DAVID *dance gently, without looking at each
other. They feel good, both are enjoying each other's silent
company. Suddenly they look in each other's eyes.* DAVID
embraces NANCY *and after briefly enjoying the embrace,
she pushes him away.*

NANCY: You're not supposed to dance this close.

> DAVID *apologises with a smile. Though he can't see
> her,* NANCY's *face reflects how much she would rather
> he did embrace her and the effort it's taking her not to
> embrace him.*

83. DIEGO'S BUILDING: PASSAGEWAY. INT. NIGHT

NANCY *and* DAVID *walking along the passage. Opposite*
DIEGO's *door,* DAVID *acts as if he's going to knock really
hard.* NANCY *enjoys holding him back. He gives her a hug
as part of the game. She moves away and they go on to
her flat. They stop in front of her door.*

NANCY: Here we are.

> DAVID *wants to go in and she wants him to.*

NANCY: It's been a really nice day, though you haven't said more than twenty words.

DAVID: But I feel so good. Yesterday I felt unhappy and today I feel so good. (*pause*) Can I come in?

> NANCY *is overwhelmed by the question. She delays her reply because she finds it difficult to say no.*

NANCY: It's getting very late. Come back tomorrow. (*Gently closes the door*)

84. NANCY'S FLAT. INT. NIGHT

NANCY *leaning against the door, hoping she'll calm down but enjoying it all the same. She looks at Santa Barbara.*

NANCY: Don't let me spoil things.

85. STUDENT RESIDENCE: SOCIAL AREA. INT. NIGHT

A group of students, MIGUEL *among them.* DAVID *comes in from the street and walks through.* MIGUEL *notices him come in.*

86. STUDENT RESIDENCE: DAVID'S ROOM. INT. NIGHT

DAVID *in his room.* MIGUEL *walks in.*

MIGUEL: Hey, are you sleeping here?

DAVID: (*Looks at him straight on*) What's it got to do with you?

MIGUEL: You're never around. I thought you must be sleeping somewhere else as well.

DAVID: I'll sleep where I want to, right?

MIGUEL: Don't think I don't know where you're going.

DAVID: What's got into you?

MIGUEL: I don't want you making an idiot out of me.

DAVID: Nobody's making an idiot out of you. Leave me in peace, Diego as well.

MIGUEL: Diego? You don't say 'the queer' now. Now he's Diego, is he? So that's the headline news. David Alvarez's championing homosexuals.

DAVID: What do you mean? I'm more of a man than ever. And 'the queer''s got more principles and value than you think.

MIGUEL: You don't say. You stood up for him? I can imagine what with.

DAVID *is annoyed by the provocation, but keeps his cool.*

DAVID: The Revolution has acted differently towards you and me. He deserves a break.

MIGUEL: Really? What's that all about? French communism or Prague Springs? (*Violently he grabs him by the arm and points to the window*). Look, 90 miles from here, we've got the enemy, and the waverers, the people that criticise, are on their side.

DAVID: (*Wriggles away*) I'm not over there. I'm here. And so is he. Why can't he be a revolutionary?

MIGUEL: Because the Revolution doesn't come in through the back entrance.

87. DIEGO'S HOUSE: PASSAGEWAY. INT. DAY
DIEGO *opposite* NANCY's *door with a dish full of jam.*

DIEGO: Nancy, Nancy. I know you're in there. Forgive me. I didn't mean to insult you. (*Knocks*). Open up.

NANCY: I won't forgive you. I'm going to commit suicide. I've left a note saying you're to blame.

DIEGO: Nancy, for heaven's sake, don't do anything foolish. Open up, I don't feel well and I don't want to be by myself.

NANCY: Your boyfriend can keep you company.

DIEGO: How can you say that, Nancy? You know you might never see me again.

NANCY *opens up. Smiles at* DIEGO, *showing that her irritation was only in jest*

NANCY: I'll do it!

DIEGO: What will you do?

NANCY: Go to bed with him.

DIEGO: No, Nancy. Forgive me. I want you to forget that.

NANCY: I'm not going to because you asked me. I'm going to do it because I want to. I want him to know what love's really like, and with me.

DIEGO *gives her a solemn look.*

DIEGO: Are you in love with him? No, Nancy, that can't be. He's very good-looking but he's too young.

NANCY *averts her gaze.*

DIEGO: For Christ's sake.

88. BOOKSHOP. INT. DAY

DAVID*'s browsing through the history and political section. Selects out books by* MARTÍ, MARX, FIDEL, LENIN. DIEGO, *in another part of the library, holding an art book, catches sight of him. Pretending to be absorbed in his book he moves into his line of vision.* DAVID *sees* DIEGO, *is embarrassed. Slips off to avoid being seen. The scene finishes on* DIEGO *who looks up sadly from his book only to see* DAVID *leaving the shop.*

89. THE DEN: SITTING-ROOM. INT. DAY

DAVID, *with a beautiful shirt that* DIEGO *has just given him. He's so grateful that he's at a loss for words. Is so pleased and happy that he doesn't know where to put himself.* DIEGO *enjoys his embarrassment.*

DIEGO: Give it a try on Sunday at the Lezama Lima lunch. I've invited your girlfriend.

DAVID *looks at him, radiant. Puts the shirt down.*

DAVID: I've also brought you something. (*He goes to his*

rucksack and takes out a photo of a youthful Fidel, *a poster of* Che, *a 26 July arm-band, things which he shows to* DIEGO). Now, aren't these things also part of Cuba?

He goes over to the Cuban Altar and adds the new symbols. As well as the aforementioned, a badge from the Literacy Campaign and a necklace of santajuana beads. DIEGO *lets him get on with it, doesn't say a word. Gets more and more depressed during the scene.*

DAVID: (*Opposite the Altar*) Now it's complete. (*Goes over to* DIEGO, *takes him by the hand and invites him to sit down*) Come here, we've got things to talk about.

DIEGO: Like Nora and Thorvald?

DAVID: Fuck Nora and Thorvald. You're always giving me books. It's my turn now. (*He hands him the books he has just bought*) I'm going to get rid of the poison in your veins. I know you've suffered, but I want you to get back into society. I'm going to help you. You're intelligent and you can't judge the Revolution on the basis of your personal experience.

DIEGO: Can't I?

DAVID: No. You must see things more widely. The Revolution isn't only what affects us. Think about my position, not yours. I'm studying in the university, and who am I? The son of peasants.

DIEGO: Like Stalin.

DAVID: I'm serious. We want to live according to our own lights, and that's what they can't forgive. It's just the same that happens to you but at a national level.

DIEGO: I can see . . .

DAVID: They're mounting a whole campaign against us, can't you understand that? Hungary in 56, and Chekoslovakia in 68, and Stalin . . . What's any of that

169

got to do with us? The Second World War was in 45, Stalin died in 53. I hadn't even been born. Why don't they remind the Americans every morning that Truman Capote dropped the atomic bomb?

DIEGO: Harry Truman. It was never Truman Capote: he was a homosexual. And don't justify Stalin with Truman.

DAVID: What I mean is that it's regrettable, but understandable, that we sometimes make mistakes, like sending Pablo to the UMAP camps. It happens in all real Revolutions.

DIEGO: Pablo and the rest. What about the poor queens who weren't singers? What kind of an education is that?

DAVID: But that belongs to the past. Diego, the mistakes aren't the Revolution. They're part of the Revolution but they are not the Revolution.

DIEGO: And who carries the can? Nobody will ever take responsibility.

DAVID: One day nobody will be more understanding than the Revolution. If not, it wouldn't be the Revolution.

DIEGO: You mean that under Communism we queers are going to be happy?

DAVID: Probably.

DIEGO: And will the day come when I can set up any exhibition I like without having to ask permission or give explanations? And what if I bump into you in a bookshop, will I be able to say hello without you being ashamed or it damaging you?

DAVID: (*Embarrassed*) OK, it won't just drop from the heavens. We'll have to struggle for it: homosexuals and those of us who aren't.

DIEGO: And till that day comes, at least between these four walls, I can give you a hug?

DAVID: You see? It really annoys me. All our conversations end on the same note. You lecture me about respecting you for what you are but you don't respect me for what I am. I don't like that.

DIEGO: All right. I wasn't talking as a man or as a homosexual. It's what I need. I feel really in a bad way.

DAVID: And why do you feel like that? Tell me? I am your friend.

90. THE DEN: SITTING ROOM. INT. DAY

The LEZAMA LIMA *lunch. It starts by day and finishes at night.*

The scene has two objectives: the meal as an experience for DAVID, *the presentation, its mouthwatering appearance, the pleasure with which the guests join in; and the relationship between* DAVID *and* NANCY *that is definitively established through looks and smiles.* DIEGO *relishes every detail but says nothing. The exchanges (simple chatter that is part of the ceremony) belong to conversations recreated from the novel* Paradiso *by* JOSÉ LEZAMA LIMA, *and will be adapted to the set. They drink Spanish wines from beautiful glasses. Rocco has been moved into the sitting-room. Cuban music throughout.*

The scene opens on the elegant table that has already been laid. First-class table cloths and crockery. DAVID, *in shirt and tie, is just putting the final touches to the glasses and then positions the candelabra in the right place.*

DAVID: Diego, come and have a look.

DIEGO *comes in from the kitchen.*

DIEGO: Perfect. Only the lady is missing.

NANCY'S VOICE: Was missing.

DAVID *turns round.* NANCY *is in the doorway, looking*

very fetching, done up for DAVID's *sake like a girl from
the country.*

NANCY and DAVID: How handsome! How pretty!

*They laugh. He goes over to her, makes her turn
round, she looks at him, they're speechless looking at
each other's finery. They're all eyes.*

91. THE DEN: SITTING-ROOM. INT. DAY

The three of them sitting at the table, NANCY *and* DAVID
on one side and DIEGO *on the other, facing the camera,
leading the proceedings. In the background, the Cuban
Altar. Light from the candelabra and some daylight slips
through the half-closed balcony shutters.*

The scene opens with DIEGO *taking the lid off the soup
tureen, where a thick plantain soup is steaming.*

DIEGO: (*Stirs the soup, serves it*) 'I wanted to rejuvenate
you, my little darlings, by taking you back to your first
childhood. That's why I added a little tapioca to the
soup . . .

DAVID: What's that?

NANCY: Yucca. Don't interrupt.

DIEGO: 'And I've floated on the top some sweet corn, one
of the many things we liked as kids yet which we've
never enjoyed since . . .'

NANCY (*Mischievously, in harmony with* DIEGO, *recites
this paragraph from memory*): 'Diego must have
prepared so much delicious fare, that we'll have to
watch out for a homespun embolism, the most deadly
of all known varieties, according to Dr . . . Santurce.'

This is a total mystery to DAVID, *but he follows the
others as they drink their soup. The gestures, looks,
relish with which they drink it down, make it clear
that the soup is delicious.*

173

92. THE DEN: SITTING-ROOM. INT. DAY

DIEGO *carries from the kitchen a tray with a soufflé. As he gives his speech, he sits down, serves etc.*

DIEGO: 'Let's change canary glitter for the graceless prawns. (*He uncovers and shows off the contents of the tray*) Time for the second course. The soufflé containing the renowned swordfish and lobsters gawping in livid panic as if their carapaces were greeting the torch that would burn out their bulging eyes.'

DAVID *still can't understand the patter being recited by* DIEGO, *but he's enjoying every detail, convinced he's participating in a mystery which will soon be revealed. They tuck into the soufflé, which tastes wonderful. The scene fades a few minutes later.*

93. THE DEN: SITTING-ROOM. INT. DAY

They have finished the soufflé and are licking their lips. As previously, DIEGO's *words accompany their actions: plates are taken away, are replaced by others,* NANCY *and* DAVID *exchange glances . . .*

DIEGO: 'After a dish that so successfully preened its strident colours, a flaming Gothic of almost Baroque proportion yet retaining the Gothic in the texture of the dough and the allegories sketched by the prawns, let some light relief into the lunch with this beetroot salad, mayonnaise dressing, Lübeck asparagus . . .'

As he serves out the salad, he drops some slices, clearly on purpose. He gives DAVID *a look of satisfaction.*

DIEGO: Such perfection. An excellent omen.

DAVID *is still at a loss but is enjoying himself.* DIEGO *signals to* NANCY. *She stops and goes into the kitchen.* DIEGO *looks enigmatically at* DAVID *while making him wait for the lady to return. She comes in with the*

*main dish. Places it in the centre of the table and takes
the lid off. A magnificent, mouthwatering stuffed
turkey appears whose delicious aroma reaches even the
spectators.* DAVID *is taken aback, and he looks up
towards* DIEGO, *who is holding a copy of* Paradiso.

DIEGO: You are present, pretty boy, at the family lunch
that doña Augusta regales in the pages of *Paradiso*, the
most glorious novel that has ever been written in this
Island. Chapter seven, Cuban edition. (*Handing him
the book*) It's a present, with the author's
unmistakable signature.

*DAVID is overwhelmed by the present. He takes the
book, opens it, leafs through it as if it were something
holy.*

DIEGO: Now you can say you've eaten like a real Cuban
and for you to join forever the ranks of the Master's
admirers, all that remains is for you to read his work.
Dissolve into . . .

94. THE DEN: SITTING-ROOM. INT. NIGHT

*The meal is over. The table's not been cleared away, and
includes cups of coffee and a box of cigars.* NANCY *reclines
like an odalisk on the sofa, drinking wine and looking at
an entranced* DAVID.

NANCY: We've dined like royalty.

*DAVID, in his role as a novice, tries to start to smoke.
He is conscious of and is enjoying NANCY's attentions
and everything he does is for her. They're both amused
by the failed attempts of the would-be smoker. The
tobacco passes to a second plane and their looks
finally meet. Then DIEGO appears, coming down from
his bedroom in a real hurry, putting his jacket on.*

DIEGO: I'm really late.

DAVID: How come you're going out?

NANCY: (*Half-heartedly*) Don't go, Diego, don't be so sad.

DIEGO: (*Picks up his bag*) I've got an important appointment. (*He takes from the cupboard a bottle of Havana Club rum and puts it on the table*) In case you feel like a drink. (*To* DAVID) Careful, it's the genuine item.

NANCY: Have you got your passport?

DIEGO *opens his eyes wide.*

DAVID: What passport?

NANCY: That's what he calls his Identity Card.

DIEGO: (*Looks at his watch*) Ciao, my pretties. (*He goes to the record-player and changes the record*) Listen to this, I was keeping it for you. (*From the doorway*) Behave yourselves, but if you're going to behave badly, wait for me. (*Exits*)

It's soothing music. DAVID *goes over to* NANCY *and asks her to dance. She doesn't wait to be asked a second time. They dance gently from one end of the living-room to the other, until they come to a halt.* NANCY, *trying to control her emotions, or looking for an excuse to avert her gaze which is betraying her, starts to tidy up the knot to his tie. He lets her get on with it.*

DAVID: I want to kiss you.

NANCY: No.

A no *which means yes.* DAVID *kisses her. They separate out.* DAVID *really liked the kiss. He looks at her, they kiss even more passionately, a long, beautiful kiss in which* NANCY *lets him take the lead. The next kiss is hers, and is slightly more intense. Then he kisses her, raising the temperature in turn. He embraces her tightly and undoes her dress straps. The kisses and dance have brought them over to the stairs and* DIEGO'S VIRGIN.

DAVID: These stairs must lead somewhere.

177

*She accepts. He takes her hand and invites her to go
upstairs. Behind* DAVID's *back* NANCY's *free hand
caresses the image of the* VIRGIN. *The music's still
playing.*

95. THE DEN: BEDROOM. INT. NIGHT
DAVID *and* NANCY *facing each other. They undress slowly,
beautifully.* NANCY *undresses first. Then she takes his shirt
off, leaving his tie on, that he has finally untied. She
doesn't take it off but pulls him gently towards the bed.
She gets into bed, draws him after her. He now takes the
initiative: they start to make love.*

NANCY: My beautiful little boy. My little man. A lovely
  Young Communist. My macho from Cumanayagua.

DAVID: I'm not from Cumanayagua.

NANCY: Such sweet lips. Such delicious breath. I'm your
  sweetheart. Take me. I want to feel you . . .
  For one moment, DAVID *stops. He looks at her rather
  frightened and shamefaced.* NANCY *opens her eyes.*

DAVID: I think I've got an attack of nerves.
  She smiles at him almost blissfully.

NANCY: Love's like that. You get attacks of nerves.
  *Delicately, she changes her position in relation to him,
  puts him beneath her. She gazes at him, caresses his
  face, chest, belly, his chest again. Kisses him on the
  lips, gently but passionately, skilfully. Bites his chin,
  runs her lips down his neck, chest, sucks a nipple,
  relaxing* DAVID *who is enjoying himself, and* NANCY
  *takes her knowing kisses further down. Her head and
  hands disappear towards* DAVID's *pubis. His face
  registers extraordinary stabs of fear and pleasure.*

96. THE DEN: SITTING-ROOM. INT. NIGHT
DIEGO's *living-room: the Cuban Altar, the poster for* Some

179

Like It Hot *etc.* DAVID *and* NANCY *make love upstairs. The sound of panting and gasping.*
The charms, clappers, mobiles and other oddments clink and stir slowly. The sound of orgasm being reached.
The music finishes. Silence.
After a while, DAVID *comes down, naked, exhausted and happy. He goes to the record-player and changes the record. Now* BENNY MORE *is singing, cheerful, full of life.* DAVID *sits at the table, with the Cuban Altar behind him. He seizes hold of a turkey drumstick left on the dish and bites into it hungrily. Takes things from other dishes and tureens. Soaks up some gravy with a piece of bread. Tries a dessert, licking the sweet taste from his finger. Wipes his mouth with the back of his hand. Pours himself a glass of rum, gulps it down. It burns his insides but relaxes him. He drinks the remains of a cup of coffee. He takes a cigar. Examines it, smells it, looks at the photo of* LEZAMA *in which he appears with a cigar in his mouth.* DAVID *tries to light his own. Succeeds at a second attempt. Sucks, rather bewildered. Likes it. Coughs and waves the smoke away. He looks at* LEZAMA's *photo and takes another puff on the cigar in the style of the master. Puts the cigar down, fills a plate with things to eat, takes the bottle of rum and goes up to the bedroom.*

97. SCHOOL OF POLITICAL SCIENCES. EXT. DAY
DAVID's *legs.* DAVID's *incredibly happy face. He's inside the university, at the top of the staircase. He looks around, master of himself and all around him. Quite unlike the previous insecure, diffident* DAVID. *He starts walking, sticking his chest out, keeping his belly in, passes in front of the Alma Mater, at whom he directs a look of satisfaction. He stops at the entrance to the school, where his companions are gathering. With a confidence and panache that are new to him, all smiles. He heads towards*

*the group, greets them, joins them. Kisses the odd female
friend on the cheek, slings his arm round the shoulder of
the odd friend, goes in the school with everyone else.*
MIGUEL *observes him from a bench. His eyes follow*
DAVID'S *final movements.*

98. THE SANTERO'S HOUSE. INT. DAY

A happy NANCY *kneeling in front of the SANTERO. Inside a
modest room with a santería decor. Statues or images of
Santa Barbara-Changó, the Virgin of Charity-Ochun, San
Lazaro Babalu, Jesus Christ. Nancy lights candles, arranges
her offerings.*

NANCY: Godfather, you see how right I was? I feel
    sweetness, purity within me . . . I am like that, I knew
    that was the real me. I'll take him to live with me. I'll
    make sure he studies, and if he goes out with girls, I'll
    turn a blind eye. (*To Santa Barbara*) Thank you,
    Changó. I've always loved you. My Godfather knows
    that, don't you? (*Her Godfather averts his gaze, looks
    serious.* NANCY *looks alarmed, looks at Santa Barbara*)
    What do my past and age matter when it comes to
    love? I do exercises, I dye my hair. And I'll tell HIM
    about my life, warts and all. (*To her Godfather*) He'll
    understand me, he'll realise that inside me is something
    clean which nobody has dirtied, and it's that bit of me
    I'm offering him. (*To the Saint, distressed*) Don't turn
    against this, Changó, don't take him away from me.
    (*To her Godfather*) Don't let him be taken away from
    me. (*To the crucifix on the wall*) Don't let him take
    him from me. (*To Santa Barbara*) Even if it's only for
    a year. (*To Jesus Christ*) Are you going to help me?
    (*She beseeches the other deities, her Godfather*) Will
    Ochun help me? Will you help me, Godfather? (*To
    them all*) Help me, for fuck's sake!

99. THE DEN: SITTING-ROOM. INT. DAY

Someone knocks at the door. DIEGO *comes and opens up.*
MIGUEL *appears in the doorway: smart, not a hair out of place, he sends* DIEGO's *way the most innocent smile in the whole film.*

MIGUEL: Diego, I presume?

> *Immediately,* DIEGO *sees* MIGUEL *as a beautiful and likely conquest. He gets flirtatious. Stares at him.*

DIEGO: Yes, for whatever his Lordship desires.

MIGUEL: I was told you take photos.

DIEGO: Photos? I take the best in all Havana. But not of anybody . . . only of models who inspire art . . . I'm entirely at your disposition.

MIGUEL: (*Accepts the compliment, smiles*) Thank you . . .

DIEGO: Of course, they'll cost . . .

MIGUEL: I can pay.

DIEGO: I'm sure you can. How could I be so rude. Come in, kid, come in. (*He moves aside, inviting him to step inside.*)

100. STREET. EXT. DAY

In an area of Old Havana, DAVID *is buying a bouquet of red flowers and one of yellow flowers.*

101. THE DEN: SITTING-ROOM. INT. DAY

MIGUEL, *on the sofa, holding a glass in his hand with a magazine on his lap. He's smoking. Opposite him the small table with the bottle of 'whisky', the ice-bucket, magazines, a plate of biscuits and strips of ham and cheese.*

MIGUEL: I want them to send to a French girlfriend of mine. (*He takes a sip*) She's back in France, but she visits regularly.

DIEGO: French women are no fools . . . (*He sits on the sofa*) I should make it clear that I only take artistic shots . . .

MIGUEL: Just what I want. Like the ones in magazines.
Shall we do them now?

DIEGO: Better than the ones in magazines. (*He gets up*) We
must create the right atmosphere and let our
imaginations get to work.

MIGUEL *nods in agreement.*

DIEGO: I'll get my camera.

As he passes behind MIGUEL *he strokes his head. As
soon as he is by himself,* MIGUEL *pours himself the
biggest glass possible and drinks it in one gulp. Puts
the glass back to where it was.*

102. NANCY'S FLAT: SITTING-ROOM. INT. DAY

NANCY, *down in the dumps, is setting out the tarot cards
on the table. She doesn't dare look at them. While she's
doing this, someone knocks gently on the door, which is
half-open.* NANCY *looks anxious, guessing that it is*
DAVID. *And it is, he stands in the doorway with the
bunch of yellow flowers chest high and a smile that is
half childish, half-mischievous.* NANCY *looks at the
flowers, looks at* DAVID. DAVID *brings out the bunch of
red flowers that he was hiding behind his back.* NANCY
breaks out in tears of joy. DAVID *goes over and embraces
her.*

103. THE DEN: SITTING-ROOM. INT. DAY

MIGUEL *posing.* DIEGO *takes a photo.* MIGUEL *enjoys
having his photo taken. He strikes another pose.* DIEGO
doesn't seem to like it.

MIGUEL: Don't you like me like that?

DIEGO: I think one with your shirt off would have the
French girl in a swoon.

MIGUEL *doesn't hesitate. Takes his shirt off.* DIEGO
stares at him quite openly.

DIEGO: Leonardo and Michelangelo are right. The male body is more beautiful than the female.

MIGUEL: Who are they?

DIEGO: Two Italian friends of mine.

MIGUEL: Have you got lots of foreign friends?

DIEGO: The ones I need in order to survive.

He takes a photo. MIGUEL, *quite naturally, eases his genitals, a gesture that doesn't escape* DIEGO, *and* MIGUEL *notices it doesn't escape him. They exchange a glance which ends with an 'innocent' smile from* MIGUEL. DIEGO *closes the balcony, half-opens the shutters looking for a lighting effect.*

DIEGO: That's right, now I see you, now I don't.

MIGUEL *strikes a pose. Makes his genitals comfortable again 'so now you see them, now you don't'.*

DIEGO: Cigarette between lips.

MIGUEL *puts it there.*

DIEGO: Now you look like a rebel without a cause.

MIGUEL: That's me. I'm a rebel, but with a cause. I really want to sell communism to you.

DIEGO: Shush, don't say that, dearie. (*He looks at him*) I think this needs a bit more sex appeal. (*He walks over*) Allow me. (*He lowers the zipper of his fly, opens up his trousers*). That's better. Put your hands behind your neck and lean against the wall.

MIGUEL *does what he is told, sticks his hips out.* DIEGO *takes a photo.*

DIEGO: (*Hands him the whisky.*) In fact my speciality is nudes. How about it? It's quite professional.

MIGUEL *looks at him, smiles, and, decisively, takes his trousers off, quite to the surprise of* DIEGO *who wasn't expecting such a quick result. He's bowled over by* MIGUEL *in underpants. Excited by his model's eagerness,* DIEGO *helps him into a pose on the sofa,*

and that allows him a bit of hands on. Just as DIEGO *is
about to take the photo, the film finishes.*

DIEGO: Wait a minute, I'll put another one in.

He sits down on a chair and starts changing the film.
MIGUEL *comes over, 'interested' in the operation. In*
DIEGO'S *line of vision we see* MIGUEL *very close, his
bulging genitals within reach. This proximity provokes*
DIEGO *who has to stop what he is doing.* MIGUEL *runs
to one side, touches the camera.*

MIGUEL: Is this the diaphragm?

*In doing this he's got so close that his genitals almost
brush against* DIEGO'S *arm. He's at the point of
losing control. There's a noise at the door and*
MIGUEL *moves away. They both look.* DAVID *and*
NANCY *are in the doorway.* DAVID *is taken aback,
reacts indignantly and few words are needed before
they come to blows.*

DAVID: You queer! Is that how you wanted to trap him?

A violent struggle between DAVID *and* MIGUEL, *to the
surprise of* DIEGO *and* NANCY, *who don't understand.
The take concentrates on the hatred with which they
fight each other, that is incomprehensible to the others.*

104. NANCY'S FLAT: SITTING-ROOM. INT. DAY

DAVID *sitting on a chair.* NANCY *is treating a wound.*
DIEGO *is really ashamed of himself, doesn't dare to look*
DAVID *in the face, who won't look at him either.*

DIEGO: David, forgive me. How could I ever imagine it
was a trap?

NANCY: Don't apologise. He came with that pretty face
wanting you to take his photograph, how were you to
know?

DIEGO: (*To* DAVID) Can he do you any harm, can he
accuse you in the university?

186

DAVID: He won't, he doesn't want to get into that. It's you he hates, not me.

NANCY: Both of you, don't be such an innocent. He must think that you two . . .

DIEGO: What the hell does it matter to him?

DAVID: He wanted to catch you at something illegal. Take you to the police, accuse you of being homosexual. *Mention of the police terrifies* DIEGO. *He turns round and rushes out.*

DAVID: Hey, where are you off to?

NANCY: Leave him, David! You're frightened and he's ashamed at what happened.

105. DIEGO'S HOUSE. EXT. DAY
Shots of the building. Dawn is breaking.

106. DIEGO'S HOUSE: PASSAGEWAY. INT. DAY
DAVID *leaves* NANCY's *flat on his way to the university. He stops opposite* DIEGO's *door. Knocks. No reply.* DAVID *is surprised. Knocks louder, instinctively worried.*

107. THE DEN: SITTING-ROOM. INT. DAY
DIEGO, *dressed to go out, looks at the door in trepidation. He's standing by the table, where there is an open folder filled with papers. When he notices the folder, he closes it and hides it away. He says nothing and waits. More knocks.* DIEGO *walks quietly over to the door without making a sound, bolts the security lock. More knocking on the door.*

108. DIEGO'S HOUSE: PASSAGEWAY. INT. DAY
DAVID *senses that the locked door is a bad omen. Walks off bemused.*

109. DIEGO'S BUILDING: STREET. EXT. DAY

Front entrance. DIEGO *looks out very warily. He looks one way, then another. He rushes out nervously with the folder under his arm and an umbrella.*

DAVID *can see* DIEGO *and goes after him.* DIEGO *turns the corner and* DAVID *has to put a move on. He catches him just as he turns down another alleyway equally mysteriously.* DAVID *follows him. Peers round cautiously. He can see an elegant diplomatic car and* DIEGO *with some diplomats he obviously knows. He gives the folder to the first diplomat. They all get into the car. The car drives past him and is soon speeding off down the main street.* DAVID *is taken aback. He feels so sick that he has to lean against the wall. His chest hurts, he looks on the point of collapse.*

110. DIEGO'S BUILDING: STREET. EXT. DAY

The rain is pelting down. DAVID *shelters and waits under an eave, sad, in despair.*

A taxi stops, DIEGO *gets out and runs into the building.* DAVID *crosses the street under the torrential rain. He also walks in.*

111. THE DEN: SITTING-ROOM. INT DAY

DIEGO *takes off his wet clothes. Loud banging on the door. He's no sooner undone the bolt than* DAVID *makes a violent entrance. He looks angry, upset and threatening.*

DAVID: I saw you getting into the diplomatic car.

> DIEGO *looks at him completely bewildered.* DAVID *storms over to the Cuban Altar and tears off the symbols that he added as well as others like the flag, the photos of Martí and Lezama, etc.* DIEGO *looks at him thunderstruck.*

188

DAVID: I always had my suspicions. Don't think you fooled me.

DIEGO: David, it's not what you're thinking.

DAVID: You're a sodding pansy. That's what you are.

DIEGO: David. (*Distraugh*) Fuck! I'm leaving. I'm leaving the country!

DAVID *stops. Looks at him.*

DIEGO: They're friends who are helping me. (*Takes a bag and extracts his passport and papers*) Look at my passport, look at my immigration papers. Have a good read. I'm leaving, they're kicking me out of the country!

DAVID: What do you mean they're kicking you out?

DIEGO: I was going to tell you, but I didn't want you to find out so quickly.

DAVID: (*Looks at the papers*) Who's kicking you out? What have you done?

DIEGO: I've done nothing. I'm queer so they sacked me.

DAVID: Why? Something must have happened.

DIEGO: Germán's exhibition, then the letters I sent. You can't imagine the effect that had. They say I was putting out propaganda, they accuse me of getting out of control.

DAVID: That's no reason for them to kick anyone out. They'll fine you.

DIEGO: Do you think it could be worse? They won't drive me to the airport, don't think it was that easy. I can no longer work in the areas I want to, and with these comments on my record, who will ever employ me, who is going to risk their neck on my behalf? I'll have to work in the countryside or on building sites, and you tell me what am I going to do with a brick, where shall I ever put it?

DAVID: I don't understand. Is German going as well?

189

DIEGO: Germán is in Mexico with the gallery consultant!

DAVID: So what?

DIEGO: I'm not Germán. I made the mistake of thinking you could say things out loud. But, no, you only want to listen to yourselves. What's good and revolutionary is what you say and that's all there is to it. Now I'm just scared. Really scared.

DAVID: Scared of what?

DIEGO: That they'll come here. I don't know who will knock on that door next.

DAVID: I'll defend you. What are you going to do? Give up your country, your city? The people helping you now will want to be repaid later on, you know that. Are you going to sign letters and speak on the radio against us, against me?

DIEGO: I'll not do that.

DAVID: Yes, you will. They'll force you.

DIEGO: You think everybody's the same. I don't want to go, David, believe me. But we only live once and I want to do things, and make plans like anyone else. Isn't that my right, for fuck's sake? I like the way I am.

DAVID: Of course. You've got lots to offer.

DIEGO: A 'queen', a degenerate who's perverting the youth, that's what you lot think of me.

DAVID: How can you leave, Diego? This is your country.

DIEGO: Right, but you people don't want me.

112. HAVANA. EXT. DAY

Different takes of the city. A melancholy, farewell tone. The last ones are from DIEGO's *perspective as he looks out from his balcony.*

190

113. THE DEN: SITTING-ROOM. INT. DAY

From inside the Den we get a back view of DIEGO *on the balcony. He suddenly turns round full of emotion, even euphoric. We still can't see* DAVID.

DIEGO: My balcony is such a heavenly spot! I don't know why it's so magical but the most handsome Havanans pass this way.

We see a serious, sad-looking DAVID *by the door. Behind him, the poster for* Some Like It Hot. *The Den has already lost much of its decoration and the bookshelves are almost empty.* DIEGO *captures* DAVID's *state of mind. He attempts to look happy and carefree.*

DIEGO: Before they come to do the inventory, take the typewriter.

He walks round the room, touches various places in the room, talks incessantly in order not to give DAVID *an opportunity to introduce sad thoughts or issues.* DAVID *listens, silent and sombre.*

DIEGO: (*Shows him a packet*) These are my photos of Old HAVANA. Keep some of them and send the rest to the City Museum. What's this? Oh, my essay on Cuban feminine poetry in the 19th century. I'll take that. No, you can have it. Did you select your records? Leave some to put them off the scent. Take that look off your face! Come on, why don't you grab your opportunity. Pull down your trousers. I warn you: I can't remember a man whose willy I've not sighted. Anyway, I can imagine what yours is like: as soft as a baby dove.

DAVID is still depressed. DIEGO picks up the tea-cups.

DIEGO: Look, I'll leave you these. And the ash tray which belonged to Lezama and a fountain pen that was Virgilio Piñera's. And what about this handkerchief?

It's Antón Arrufat's, keep it (*affectionately ironic*) in case some day he becomes famous.

DAVID: I want to leave with you.

DIEGO: (*Moved by the suggestion*) No, David. You're not to blame for the fact they're kicking me out.

DAVID: Yes, I am. I can't defend you. I don't know what to do or where to go. But that's not why. I want to take you out. Let's go early and you can take me to your favourite places in Havana. I'll pay. I've got money.

DIEGO *looks at him hesitant and touched.*

DAVID: Please.

DIEGO: All right. Let's invite Nancy.

DAVID: Just you and me. (*Half-joking*) This is men's business.

114. CASABLANCA. EXT. DAY

The Christ. DAVID *and* DIEGO *sitting at the foot of the Christ. They look at the view which we still can't see.*

DIEGO: This is the best view of all. Isn't it wonderful? I'll make you a present of this look-out point. You and Nancy.

DAVID *contemplates the view in ecstasy. We see the view: Havana as seen from the Christ, a really extraordinary sight.*

DIEGO'S VOICE: Let me have a good look. It's my last.

DAVID'S VOICE: Why will it be your last?

DIEGO'S VOICE: (*Ironically*) Do you think this is going to collapse?

DAVID'S VOICE: No, but we'll stop being such brutes.

DIEGO *and* DAVID. *They're silent for a moment. They're really sad and are trying to hide the fact.*

DIEGO: As I've only been seen with you recently, guess what my enemies call me? The Red 'Queen'.

DAVID *smiles.*

193

DIEGO: Some people think that my departure is just a ploy, that I'm really off to Mata Hari it in Europe.

DAVID: After all that you never told me how you became a queer.

DIEGO: If I tell you, you'd be gone in a flash. Tell me: your first sexual experience, your erotic dreams. Don't think you can trick me: with those cute eyes you must be fireworks in bed.

DAVID: If only you knew . . .

DIEGO: Tell me, come on.

DAVID: You'll never believe this. Nancy was my first woman.

DIEGO: (DIEGO *is astonished*) Impossible. Someone as attractive as you? I don't believe that.

DAVID: Listen to me. I bet you can't guess where it happened?

DIEGO: In Nancy's flat, I bet.

DAVID: In the Den. In your bed.

DIEGO: You cheeky pair!

DAVID *smiles, amused at* DIEGO's *disgust*.

DAVID: Why did you think of the photos in Coppelia?

DIEGO: (*Smiles*) It's an old trick. (*Pause*) Now what are you going to do?

DAVID: What do you mean?

DIEGO: With Nancy.

DAVID: We like each other a lot. She's really nice.

DIEGO: Nancy is a baby sparrow, David. She seems very strong, very alive, but she's a little sparrow. She's my most valuable present to you. Take care of her, she's very delicate. Whoever hurts her, will have God to answer to.

DAVID: Nobody will hurt her. She's with me now. Diego, you can't imagine how delicious it is being with a woman.

194

DIEGO *acts up as if he is being sick.* DAVID *is amused and gives him a friendly nudge.*

115. THE STREET. EXT. DAY
DAVID and DIEGO leave the Bunny Rabbit restaurant and walk along the pavement. DAVID puts his arm round DIEGO's shoulders. They're happy and joking. A big MULATTO who, if she's sure of anything in life it is that she's a bit of alright with a sexy walk, comes along the pavement. DIEGO stops and moves to one side to make way for her, and with effeminate tone and gestures, says to her:
DIEGO: Bye-bye, sweetie pie, big momma. Oh to be a raindrop and fall on you.
The MULATTO *looks at him in terror and rushes on just in case.*
DIEGO: Traumatised her for the rest of her life.
DAVID *laughs heartily.*

116. COPPELIA. INT. DAY
The table where DAVID *and* DIEGO *met.* DIEGO *is sitting down.* DAVID *is standing up with the dishes of ice-cream, one chocolate, the other strawberry. He's going to give* DIEGO *the strawberry but then changes his mind and gives it to himself while giving the chocolate to* DIEGO. DIEGO *accepts the change and looks at him really lovingly.* DAVID *sits down. They start to eat their ice-creams.*
DAVID: (*Slightly mannered*) Dee-li-cious! It's the only decent thing they make in this country.
DIEGO *smiles.* DAVID *glances at him the way one imagines* DIEGO *looks at him and returns to his ice-cream.*
DAVID: Ooh, a strawberry! Today's my lucky day. Anyone want it?
DIEGO *is enjoying this.* DAVID *has really found a*

strawberry. He lifts it to his mouth as DIEGO *would do, with lots of flourish.* DIEGO *is smiling broadly, very happy.*

DIEGO: You're so beautiful, honey. Your only defect is that you're not queer.

DAVID *gives up the game. Looks at him affectionately, shrugs his shoulders, says:*

DAVID: Nobody is perfect.

117. DEN: SITTING-ROOM

DAVID *and* DIEGO *in the* Den, *sitting on the floor.* DIEGO *pours into their glasses the last of the rum. Takes his glass.*

DIEGO: (*He takes off the chain that is round his neck and hands it to* DAVID) Give this to Nancy. And as soon as I've finished what I have to say to you, leave. I want no more goodbyes. I forbid you to come to the airport. (*Pause*) I'm not as noble as you think, David. The day we met in Coppelia, I was with Germán. We made a bet that I would fish you and get you into bed. It was a dollar bet. I accepted because otherwise I'd never have dared speak to you. Spilling the coffee over you, was part of the plan. Your shirt on the balcony was my victory sign. Naturally, Germán has got it around, even more now he hates me. (*Pauses, looks him deep in the eyes*) I've often said one thing and meant another. That's why I wanted a hug. I thought a hug would help me forget I've been two-faced even with a person I like so much. I thought that if I hugged you you would feel I was sorry and I would feel better. I love you so much, David. What can I ever do? Will you forgive me?

They look at each other silently. The sound of an aeroplane taking off begins to be heard in crescendo. DAVID *stands up.* DIEGO *realises he wants to give him a hug, and also stands up. They give each other a big hug.*

A NOTE ON THE EDITOR/TRANSLATOR

Peter Bush has translated the work of Chico Buarque, Juan Goytisolo and Juan Carlos Onetti. He is Reader in Literary Translation at Middlesex University for that part of the week when he's not translating. He edits *In Other Words*, the journal of the Translators Association. In the belief that literary translation is not simply a solitary, sedentary occupation, he has also been involved in Channel Four documentaries in Brazil, Cuba, Morocco, Spain and Uruguay.

FURTHER REFERENCES

Michael Chanan   *The Cuban Image* (1985)
Tomás Gutiérrez Alea   *The Viewer's Dialectic*, translated
                        by Julia Lesage, (1988)
                        The screenplay of *Memories of
                        Underdevelopment*, Edmundo
                        Desnoes's *Inconsolable Memories*
                        with an introduction by Michael
                        Chanan, (1990)
José Lezama Lima   *Paradiso* (1966) English translation
                        by Gregorio Rabassa (1974)
Paul Julian Smith   'The Language of Strawberry',
                        Sight and Sound, (December 1994)

The video of *Strawberry and Chocolate* is distributed by
Tartan Video, 79 Wardour Street, London W1V 3TH
Tel. 0171 436 5975

The documentary, *Tales from Havana: Alea's Cuba*, directed
by Alex Anderson, (1993) is available from Bandung Limited,
Block H, Carker's Lane, 53–79 Highgate Road, London
NW5 1TL. Tel. 0171 482 5045